Nadav Shragai

The "Al-Aksa is in Danger" Libel:
The History of a Lie

 Jerusalem Center for Public Affairs

© 2012 Jerusalem Center for Public Affairs
13 Tel Hai Street, Jerusalem, Israel
Tel. 972-2-561-9281 Fax. 972-2-561-9112
Email: jcpa@netvision.net.il
www.jcpa.org

Academic Editor: Eyal Meron
Translator: David Hornik
Production Director: Tommy Berzi
Managing Editor: Mark Ami-El
Graphic Design: Studio Rami & Jaki - www.ramijaki.co.il

Front Cover Photo: The Southern Wall of the Temple Mount, the Al-Aksa
Mosque with its grey dome, and the golden Dome of the Rock seen from
the south. Photo: Tommy Berzi
Back Cover Photo: Muslim worshippers gather for the breaking of the
Ramadan fast next to the Al-Aksa Mosque on October 8, 2007. AP Photo:
Kevin Frayer
Pp. 8-9 Aerial Photo: City of David, Ancient Jerusalem archive

ISBN: 978-965-218-102-2

To my wife Bat Tzion and our children: Yoav, Adi, Yael, Ariel, and Yuval

Contents

For Zion's sake will I not hold my peace,
and for Jerusalem's sake I will not rest.
(Isaiah 62:1)

Legend

1. Dome of the Rock
2. Al-Aksa Mosque
3. Mughrabi Gate
4. Mughrabi Gate Access Ramp
5. Ohel Yitzchak Synagogue
6. Hurva Synagogue
7. Western Wall of Temple Mount
8. Entrance to the Western Wall Tunnel Complex
9. Archeological excavations at the foot of the Western Wall
10. Archeological excavations at the foot of the Southern Wall
11. Southern Wall of Temple Mount
12. Eastern Wall of Temple Mount
13. Solomon's Stables (Marwani Mosque)
14. Shiloach Pool
15. City of David
16. Hulda Gates (Double Gate)
17. Exit from Western Wall Tunnel
18. Via Dolorosa
19. Jewish Quarter
20. Muslim Quarter
21. Temple Mount
22. Area G
23. Western Wall Tunnel
24. Hasmonean Channel
25. Herodian drainage channel
26. Underground passageway to the Western Wall Tunnel
27. Hezekiah's Tunnel and Gihon Spring

[9]

Prologue

"Al-Aksa is in danger" is a classic libel that was embroidered in the first half of the twentieth century against the Jewish people, the Zionist movement, and, eventually, the State of Israel. The state and its institutions—so, in brief, the libel claims—are scheming and striving to destroy the mosques on the Temple Mount and build in their stead the Third Temple. The longer the libel lives, its delusive variants striking root, the more its blind and misled devotees proliferate. The libel is ramifying, taking hold of the academic, religious, and public discourse of the Arab, Palestinian, and Muslim world as if it were pure truth. Absurdly, it strikes at the Jewish people and the State of Israel precisely in the place where the Jewish state has made the most generous gesture, the greatest concession, ever made by one religion to another—on the Temple Mount, the holiest place of the Jewish people and only the third place in importance for the Muslim religion.

The libel greatly intensifies fear and hatred between the State of Israel and the Arab world, and between Jews and Muslims all over the world. It also well serves those who initiated it, or in recent decades have carefully cultivated it, and it seems also to offer the best proof of the well-known adage that if a lie is repeated often enough, it is accepted as truth.

We will consider the sources, motivations, and various manifestations of the libel, and later go on to refute it. First, it is worth surveying three recent events that illustrate how extensively the libel has been disseminated and how widespread are the fears that stem from it among the Palestinian leadership, the Muslim masses, and the Muslim elite.

In December 2000, only two months after the outbreak of the Second Intifada, Mahmoud Abu Samra, an intelligence officer at the rank of colonel in the Fatah movement,[1] sent a letter to his president, Yasser Arafat, who at that time ruled from the Mukata compound in Ramallah. Abu Samra, who was then head of a body called the Jerusalem Center for Information, Research and Documentation, requested that Arafat be apprised of a "Zionist plan to destroy the Al-Aksa Mosque with an artificial earthquake."[2]

"Military and American reports that were recently published by the newspaper *Arab Star*," wrote Abu Samra to Arafat,

> say that an Israeli committee was formed whose members were scientists from these places: the Haifa Technion, the Weizmann Institute in Rehovot, and the Negev Institute in Beersheba. This committee authored a plan to destroy the Al-Aksa Mosque without leaving a fingerprint by means of: a. creating an artificial earthquake; b. using colliding sound waves (which come from outside a wall and push it inward); c. using the creation of an aerial vacuum; d. creating artificial local lightning storms.

Abu Samra added:

> Most of the experiments were conducted already in 1999 under the waters of the Dead Sea and also in the Negev desert. The reports point to the fact that the underground foundation of the mosque has been hollowed out by the Israeli [archeological] excavations. The Zionist experts expect the structure to collapse as a result of damage to the balance between the external air pressure and the internal pressure. I request your guidance and instructions.

Abu Samra's letter was found by Israel while taking control of Orient House in eastern Jerusalem during the 2002 anti-terror Defensive Shield operation. The letter also bears an inscription by Arafat affirming that it had reached its target. Arafat, it turns out, related to Abu Samra's report in full seriousness. He ordered in writing[3] that the information be conveyed to a group of people including eastern Jerusalem leader Faisal al-Husseini, Sheikh Yusuf Salama, member of the Palestinian cabinet Ziad Abu Ziad, and the governor of the Jerusalem district of the Palestinian Authority, Jamal Otman.

December 2000. Letter from Palestinian intelligence officer Col. Mahmoud Abu Samra to President Yasser Arafat accusing Israel of planning "to destroy the Al-Aksa Mosque by creating an artificial earthquake." Arafat ordered that the letter be distributed to key Palestinian leaders in eastern Jerusalem.

The second event, seemingly of marginal significance, was made public by Dr. Hillel Cohen in his book *Kikar Hashuk Rekah*[4] but did not attract much notice. It occurred in April 2006 and well illustrates with what ease one can assemble masses of Muslim believers to "protect the Temple Mount from the Jews" without voicing even a single cry of incitement. At the time the incident occurred, a new computerized public address system had been installed at the Al-Aksa Mosque and the muezzin Nagi al-Kazaz was recorded making the call to prayer. The system was programmed such that if, because of a delay, the muezzin did not make the call to prayer, it would function automatically and al-Kazaz's voice would be heard by many.

However, the Jewish engineer who programmed the system for the Wakf did not know the Muslim prayer hours, and the call to the noon prayers was mistakenly set for the hour of 12:45 a.m. And indeed at that hour, on the first night after the system was installed, the voice of the muezzin was suddenly heard summoning the believers to prayer. Thousands of residents of the Old City and its surroundings, who heard the call and knew this was not the prayer hour, assumed it was a call to go and defend the Temple

Mount. Many came to the place, some armed with sticks. Only after extensive efforts did the Wakf guards succeed to explain the error to them and send them home.

The third incident is also seemingly trivial, but it too illustrates the extent to which Israeli rule of the Temple Mount mosques affects millions of Muslim believers all over the world, some of them thousands of miles distant, and from what sensitive soil grow the beliefs, feelings, as well as distortions and libels concerning the mount. This story was told to the Middle East scholar Prof. Yitzchak Reiter by an Egyptian intellectual at a conference in Amman in 2000.[5]

"We are modern Muslims who do not keep the basic commandments, and we were never really religious," the Egyptian intellectual said, but

> last year, at the end of the first year of mourning for my father, my mother, who had already reached an exalted age, requested to carry out the Haj [pilgrimage to Mecca] commandment....When we stayed for a night at the court of the Kabaa [the most holy Muslim site, in Mecca], sermonizers and preachers appeared one after another. One of them began to speak about Al-Haram al-Sharif [the Exalted Holy Place, as Muslims call the Temple Mount] in Jerusalem; he discussed the place's importance to Islam, the history of Jerusalem, and the fact that in the past the site fell into the hands of the Crusaders and was liberated by Saladin. Finally, he spoke at length about the current situation of Al-Haram al-Sharif, which is under Israeli occupation. As the sermonizer's description progressed, I noticed that the listeners were seized by great emotion, and some even broke out in bitter cries. Even I and my mother, who a few years earlier had visited Al-Haram al-Sharif, which was familiar to us in reality and not just as the sermonizer depicted it, were swept away in emotion and tears flowed from our eyes. For us that was the most moving event of the pilgrimage to Mecca.[6]

Abu Samra's letter to Arafat and Arafat's reference to the "Zionist plan to destroy the Al-Aksa Mosque by creating an artificial earthquake"; the thousands who gathered to "protect the Temple Mount" on hearing the recording of the muezzin that was mistakenly played in the middle of the night; and the tears that flowed from the eyes of the Egyptian intellectual in Mecca, when confronting the supposedly grim fate of Al-Haram al-Sharif under Israeli occupation, are a kind of introduction to the story of the "Al-Aksa is in danger" libel.

Today the libel permeates the masses of Muslim believers through caricatures, films, children's stories, quizzes, sermons, print and Internet publications, ceremonies, demonstrations, and religious and purportedly academic literature, but primarily through the altering of the Muslim narrative about Jerusalem, the creation of a new Muslim myth about the city, and a redating of its history. The second main element of this new narrative is the denial of the Jewish connection to the places that are sacred to them in the Land of Israel in general and in Jerusalem and on the Temple Mount in particular. This denial is now the central theme of the discourse on Jerusalem in the contemporary Muslim world.

Muslims worshipping on the Temple Mount in the month of Ramadan, 1992. Under Israeli rule full religious freedom is maintained on the mount. (Moshe Milner, Government Press Office)

Acknowledgments

I would like to thank some institutions and individuals who assisted me in the process of gathering the materials for this book: the Israel Antiquities Authority, the Western Wall Heritage Foundation, Palestinian Media Watch, MEMRI (the Middle East Media Research Institute), archives of daily newspapers, the National Library, and staff of the library at Yad Ben Zvi. Special gratitude is owed to Brig.-Gen. Shalom Harari; to Shuka Dorfman, director-general of the Antiquities Authority; and to the rabbi of the Western Wall and the holy places, Rabbi Shmuel Rabinovich. The latter two opened many doors for me in my quest for the truth. The sources I made use of appear in the footnotes throughout the book, but three works were particularly important: *Milchamot Hamekomot Hakedushim* (The Wars over the Holy Places) by Dr. Shmuel Berkovitz; *M'Yerushalayim l'Meka v'Chazarah* (From Jerusalem to Mecca and Back) by Prof. Yitzchak Reiter; and my book *Har Hamerivah: Hama'avak al Har Habayit—Yehudim v'Muslimim, Dat v'Politika* (The Temple Mount Conflict). My close acquaintance with the issue of the Temple Mount, which I dealt with for years in journalistic and research capacities including visits to the place, has helped me in writing this book.

Unlike other publications that helped me build this book's foundations, this book's focus is on the "Al-Aksa is in danger" libel, and it adds new layers to previous discussions of this issue. Hence the book touches only lightly on some important topics connected to the subject of the Temple Mount, and only to give background knowledge on how the "Al-Aksa is in danger" libel developed. I also relied heavily on an array of publications about the archeology of Jerusalem. Worthy of note are books and articles by Prof. Dan Bahat, Dr. Eilat Mazar, Dr. Gabriel Barkai, Prof. Ronny Reich, Dr. Gideon Avni, and Tamar Winter.

Special thanks are due to Prof. Yitzchak Reiter, who read the manuscript and offered valuable comments, and whose scholarly publications were very useful to me; to Dr. Gabriel Barkai, who also read the manuscript, preempted some errors, and provided insightful comments; and to Dr. Eyal Meron, the scientific editor, who spared no effort in putting the book on firm and suitable foundations. I would also like to thank the publisher, the Jerusalem Center for Public Affairs, and particularly its president Dr. Dore Gold, and its director, Chaya Herskovic, whose comments were so helpful and illuminating, as well as Tommy Berzi, the production director of the book. Of course, the responsibility for what is written is mine alone.

Introduction

This book centers on the modern blood libel "Al-Aksa is in danger"—its roots, attributes, and various manifestations. The libel is directed at the State of Israel, the Zionist movement, and the Jewish people. It has become integral to the Muslim, Arab, and Palestinian discourse, accepted by very large numbers as the absolute truth. This book refutes the libel, clarifies its purposes, and warns of the many dangers it poses to relations between Jews and Muslims.

Roots of the Lie

The "Al-Aksa is in danger" libel posits that the State of Israel is working to achieve the collapse of the Temple Mount mosques and build the Third Temple in their stead.[1] The roots of the calumny go back to the days of the Grand Mufti of Jerusalem, Haj Amin al-Husseini, during the 1920s and 1930s, but it has become significantly vitalized in recent years and prevails in the Muslim, Arab, and Palestinian domains.

Inversion of the Truth

Some of the libel's agents worldwide also use it in the context of the envisioned global Islamic caliphate, whose capital is Jerusalem. This is a vision that threatens numerous countries in Europe, where many Muslim immigrants have recently gone to live. And yet:

1. The calumny that Al-Aksa is endangered is not only groundless. It is, in fact, precisely on the Temple Mount, the most sacred place for the Jewish people and only the third in sanctity for the Muslim religion, that the State of Israel made the greatest concession ever by one religion to another when it relinquished the exercise of the Jewish right to prayer at the location and entrusted its management to the Wakf (Muslim religious endowment) authorities.

2. Over the years the status quo that was established on the Temple Mount in 1967 has eroded to the detriment of the Jewish side. Currently, even Jewish visits to the mount are restricted, while the Muslim prayer areas have expanded appreciably.

3. Furthermore, throughout history the religions and peoples who conquered Jerusalem destroyed the houses of worship of their predecessors and retrofitted them as houses of worship for their own use. That is how Muslims and Christians treated each other when Jerusalem passed from hand to hand.[2] And, for nearly nineteen hundred years,[3] both Muslims and Christians denied the Jews access to their most holy place—the Temple Mount. In contrast, when Israel conquered the Old City of Jerusalem in 1967, it left the compound under Muslim religious

management and made only a minute correction to the historical iniquity: awarding Jews (and members of other religions) access to the mount, but simultaneously denying their rights to pray there and entrusting only the Western Wall to Jewish management.

Israel Conducts No Excavations under the Temple Mount

Since 1967, the claim that the Al-Aksa Mosque (or the whole compound) was in danger has been voiced every time that Israel has conducted archeological excavations or construction in the vicinity of the Temple Mount. Almost always the complaint has been accompanied by severe incitement, warning that Israel aimed to destroy Al-Aksa (the third most important place of worship in Islam) and summoning the believers to come and physically protect the mosque. On many occasions such incitement has produced disorders and violent incidents.

However, an examination of Muslim claims regarding eight major archeological sites within a radius of a kilometer from the Temple Mount reveals that these charges have no basis in reality.

Furthermore, throughout all the years it has ruled over united Jerusalem and its holy sites, Israel has carefully avoided conducting archeological digs under the mount. The excavations have taken place alongside the walls of the mount, or at a distance of scores or hundreds of meters from these walls. Only on one occasion, in 1981, did an excavation verge under the mount and even then its objective was not, of course, to topple the mosques. This excavation was halted at the behest of Prime Minister Menachem Begin and the original status was restored.

Manifestations of the Libel

Yet, even though the "Al-Aksa is in danger" libel is totally ludicrous, and some of its disseminators know it, today millions of Muslims throughout the world accept it as the truth, and the response to it has long exceeded any rational boundaries. The manifestations of the libel are manifold and severe, and they greatly intensify hatred, fear, and enmity between Israel and the Arab world.

Often the libel involves severe incitement, with threats of *jihad*, war, and bloodshed. Cartoons show snakes and octopuses decorated with Jewish symbols enfolding the mosque or climbing on top of it. Sometimes the libel depicts Jews in the spirit of *Der Stürmer*, digging like mice or weasels under the Temple Mount mosques. Israel has been accused of seeking to create an artificial earthquake that will level the mosques. Senior Muslim or Palestinian clerics or statesmen periodically announce that they will not hesitate to "sacrifice innocent and pure blood" to protect Al-Aksa or even commit martyrdom themselves in the face of the danger. The libel incorporates explicit anti-Semitic motifs, including some appropriated from *The Protocols of the Elders of Zion*, regarding Jewish plots to take over not only Palestine but the entire world.

Israel Prevents Damage to the Mosques, Yet Is Accused of Damaging Them

The height of absurdity is reached when Israel's security authorities, who work unceasingly to protect the Temple Mount mosques and their integrity, are often accused of abetting and even initiating actions aimed at harming the mosques. Examples include the fire at Al-Aksa in 1969, or Alan Goodman's shooting attack on the mount in 1982. Such incidents, spawned by Jewish or Christian extremists whom the State of Israel arrests, tries, and imprisons, are exploited by Muslims to organize massive fundraising campaigns for the mosques and their courtyards and to incite against Israel and the Jewish people.

Many Muslims do not distinguish between the State of Israel, whose governmental arms do everything to protect the Temple Mount mosques, and extreme, marginal Jewish actors who seek to damage them. They conflate the extremists with legitimate efforts to foster awareness of the Temple Mount (devoid of any intentions to harm the mosques). This view has no basis in reality. The result is a mélange of wild fantasies, historical distortions, and politically motivated fraud.

Agents of the Libel

The clear inheritor of the Grand Mufti, who devised the "Al-Aksa is in danger" libel eighty years ago, is the head of the northern branch of the Israeli Islamic Movement, Sheikh Raed Salah. He and his movement are responsible for the significant physical alterations on the Temple Mount since 1967: the building of two giant new underground mosques at the southeastern corner of the mount, in Solomon's Stables, and in the recesses of the passage of the Hulda Gates. The latter, built under the Al-Aksa Mosque itself, is also called "ancient Al-Aksa."

Salah has often called for "sacrificing lives to defend Al-Aksa" and uses idioms such as "our blood is still on their clothes, on their doors, in their food and drink," and "bread soaked in the blood of children." He calls for the establishment of a global Islamic caliphate whose capital is Jerusalem. Salah shares this dream or parts of it with actors such as Hamas, Hizbullah, Al-Qaeda, and the Iranian regime, which also disseminate the libel that Al-Aksa is in danger.

Salah's claim that Israel is intending to destroy the mosque and build the Third Temple in its stead was rejected by the Or Commission, a panel that Israel established to investigate the October 2000 disturbances on the mount and elsewhere. Regarding Salah, the commission wrote, among other things: "His statements on this matter were intended to garner political capital, recruit supporters and accentuate struggles....He acted to stir up the Arab public against a supposed intention of the Israeli government to replace the Al-Aksa mosques[4] with a Jewish Temple—an intention that had no connection whatsoever to reality."[5]

These statements by the commission, which included an Israeli Arab justice, apply as well to many others who propagate the libel and incitement. For instance, former Member of Knesset Abd al-Malik Dehamshe expressed his willingness to be the first martyr in defense of Islam's holy places in Jerusalem, lauding "souls...yearning to die a martyr's death for the sake of defending Al-Aksa and blessed Jerusalem."[6]

The Purpose of the Libel

The purpose of the libel, first aired in the 1920s, has been and remains to enhance Jerusalem and the Temple Mount in the Muslim and Palestinian myth, unite the Muslim world around this motif, and to exalt the status of Palestinian and Arab clerics and political leaders who make regular use of it. Salah himself admitted that his use of the libel has opened many doors for him and his movement, describing his involvement with these matters as not only essential but also instrumental. Indeed, the frequency and intensity with which the libel is raised has transformed it into factual truth for millions of Muslims.

Israel's Mild Approach

A comparison between the measures Western countries such as the United States and Britain, or Muslim states such as Jordan, Egypt, and Saudi Arabia, have taken against incitement in mosques, and the way Israel treats incitement in the Temple Mount mosques, reveals that Israel practices extreme liberality and forbearance toward Muslim clerics on the mount. It does so despite severe incitement to violence against the Jewish people, the Zionist movement, and the State of Israel that issues from these mosques.

The Al-Aksa Mosque Courtyards as a Terror Base

The "Al-Aksa is in danger" libel, the summons to come and defend it even at the sacrifice of one's life, and the language used to make the messages even more extreme have occasionally resulted in the Temple Mount mosques being employed for actual terror purposes. Over the years a number of terrorist squads have used these mosques to plan deadly attacks. One example is the Silwan squad, who in 1986 threw hand grenades at Israeli soldiers near the Dung Gate in the Old City. Others include the abductors and murderers of three policemen during 1992-1993, and the squad that in 2008 planned to set up an infrastructure for Al-Qaeda and even to shoot down President Bush's helicopter during his visit to Jerusalem. The Temple Mount and its mosques also were used for purposes of terror and violence in the First and Second Intifadas. While this activity was not, of course, coordinated with the local religious authorities, in the atmosphere of incitement the terror activists felt themselves at home.

Rewriting the History of Jerusalem

In recent years the "Al-Aksa is in danger" libel has been interwoven with the reconstruction of the Arab-Islamic case for Jerusalem. This is achieved by rewriting the Islamic and Arab history of the city. The new narrative centers on claims that the Arabs ruled Jerusalem for many years before the Jewish people's arrival, and that the Al-Aksa Mosque was built before the establishment of the Temple. This has gone hand in hand with the total negation of the Jewish-Zionist narrative concerning Jerusalem and the Temple Mount, including the de-Judaization of the mount, the Western Wall, and Jerusalem in general, and the denial that the Temple even existed.

These new narratives totally contradict what modern research knows about the Jewish and Muslim history of Jerusalem as well as what the Muslims themselves have documented in their writings over the past few hundred years.

Muslim Construction Has Endangered the Temple Mount

Over the past decade, after years in which Islamic bodies throughout the world have accused Israel of trying to cause the collapse of the Temple Mount mosques, a tangible danger of collapse of the southeastern portion of the mount and damage to the Al-Aksa Mosque has been created precisely by copious Muslim building activity in this part of the mount, along with the renovating of Solomon's Stables to serve as an underground mosque.

Ironically, the Muslims at first denied this danger, and also placed many obstacles in the path of the Israeli authorities who attempted to deal with it. At the same time, the handling of ancient recesses, revealed over the years by Israeli archeological excavations under Arab residential areas of the Old City, in many cases saved the homes above from sinking and collapsing. Crooked domes, on which entire residential areas leaned, received support. Cesspools that drained waste into these cavities and ancient halls were replaced with sewage systems.

In certain cases some of the homeowners, when asked to consent to the Israeli authorities rehabilitating (gratis) the sewage and sanitation systems that undermined the foundations of their homes, made this consent conditional on a comprehensive renewal of their homes and apartments. In effect, these homeowners extorted the Israeli authorities in return for their consent to install proper sewage systems that would prevent damage to their homes as well as to antiquities and cultural treasures buried below.

Muslim Religious Officials Have Attacked Israel Publicly and Praised It in Secret

Over the years delegations of Muslim clerics, including the heads of the Wakf and the Supreme Muslim Council, visited the archeological excavations along the Western Wall and the Southern Wall, surreptitiously. In fact, their reactions on those occasions were positive and totally contradicted the public attacks on Israel and accusations of aiming to topple the Temple Mount mosques. During these visits the Muslim religious leaders expressed fear that their positions would be exposed to the public. In at least one case, a Muslim professional lost his job after publicly expressing his favorable evaluation of the Israeli excavations.

Israel's Archeological Excavations Are an Illustrious Scientific and Cultural Endeavor

The archeological excavations that Israel has conducted over the years in the vicinity of the Temple Mount are an illustrious scientific and cultural project, done with professional and engineering supervision as well as strict safety precautions. The excavations took place openly, and experts from various fields throughout the world—including UNESCO[7] personnel—visited them. The results of these excavations have allowed devotees of culture, science, and religion, and members of all communities, Jews, Christians, and Muslims alike, to study them, identify with them, and bond with their past. The Israeli archeologists' work has also contributed significantly to the knowledge and study of the golden age of Islam in Palestine. Especially noteworthy is the discovery of the palaces of the Umayyad Dynasty south of the Temple Mount. It is, however, most natural that Israel, the state of the Jewish people, has not remained indifferent to findings from ancient periods that coincide with Jewish historical sources and religious writings, and that such findings have had an impact on the public.

The Israeli Relinquishment of the Temple Mount

The most relevant factual basis for disproving the "Al-Aksa is in danger" libel is, as noted, the de facto Israeli relinquishment of the Temple Mount, for which I could find no precedent in any other country or religion. The birthfather of this relinquishment, which for years has been called "the status quo on the Temple Mount," was Moshe Dayan, who served as Israeli defense minister during the Six-Day War. The thrilling liberation of the Western Wall and the Temple Mount was documented in detail in dozens of publications that appeared after the war. Even the cry of paratroop commander Mordechai Gur into his field radio—"The Temple Mount is in our hands!"—entered the pantheon of national symbols of the State of Israel. And yet, the reality that Israel devised on the Temple Mount, and the heavy limitations it imposed on itself there, were very far from the euphoria of the liberation itself and the overwhelming encounter with the place where the two Temples of the Jewish people had stood in the past, long the focal point of its spiritual life.

After the Six-Day War, the reality that Israel devised on the Temple Mount, and the heavy limitations it imposed on itself there, contravened in many ways everything that believing Jews pray for every day.

The reality that the State of Israel created at the site indeed contravened in many ways everything that believing Jews, keepers of the Torah and the commandments, pray for and mention in their prayers every day: "that the Temple be rebuilt speedily in our days....And there we will serve You in reverence, as in the days of old and as in former years."[1]

Dayan's first act on the Temple Mount, only a few hours after IDF Chief Rabbi Shlomo Goren blew the shofar and gave the *Shehecheyanu* blessing beside the Western Wall, was to immediately remove the Israeli flag that the paratroopers had raised on the mount.[2]

Dayan's second act was to clear out the paratroop company that was supposed to remain permanently stationed in the northern part of the mount. Dayan rejected the insistent pleas of the head of Central Command, Uzi Narkiss, who tried to prevent him from taking this measure. Narkiss reminded Dayan that Jordan, too, had stationed a military contingent on the mount to maintain order, and that long ago the Romans had done the same, deploying a garrison force in the Antonia Fortress that Herod had built near the mount. But Dayan was not persuaded. He told Narkiss that it seemed to him the place would have to be left in the hands of the Muslim guards.[3]

Despite harsh criticism from religious and nationalist circles,[4] Dayan, just a few hours after his first public announcement to the Israeli people about the holy places and particularly the Temple Mount, succinctly stated: "We have returned to the holiest of our places, never to be parted from them again….We did not come to conquer the sacred sites of others or to restrict their religious rights, but rather to ensure the integrity of the city and to live in it with others in fraternity."[5]

Here Dayan behaved as the successor of David Ben-Gurion, who already during the War of Independence in July 1948, when it appeared that the Jewish forces were about to conquer the Old City, ordered David Shaltiel, Haganah commander in Jerusalem, to "prepare a special force, loyal and disciplined…that will use without mercy a machinegun against any Jew who tries to rob or desecrate a holy place, Christian or Muslim." Ben-Gurion also recommended that Shaltiel mine the entrances to the holy places so as to prevent harm to them.[6]

Nineteen years later, a few hours after Dayan's decision, he summoned Prime Minister Levi Eshkol and the heads of the religious communities, and promised them that the places that were holy to them would not be harmed. Eshkol, for his part, announced to the chief rabbis of Israel that they would be responsible for arrangements in the vicinity of the Western Wall, and promised the religious leaders of the Christian and Muslim communities that they would continue to determine the arrangements at the places holy to them: the Church of the Holy Sepulchre and the Temple Mount.

Moshe Dayan's most significant act on the Temple Mount, which was widely criticized, was to forbid Jewish prayer there, unlike the arrangements at the Machpelah Cave in Hebron where there is also a functioning mosque.

Dayan's most significant act on the Temple Mount, which sparked controversy over the years and was widely criticized, was to forbid Jewish prayer and worship there, unlike the arrangements that emerged at the Machpelah Cave in Hebron where there is also a functioning mosque.[7] Dayan decided to leave the mount and its management in the hands of the Muslim Wakf, while at the same time insisting that Jews would be able to visit it (but not pray at it!) without restriction. Dayan thought, and years later even committed the thought to writing, that since for Muslims the mount is a "Muslim prayer mosque" while for Jews it is no more than "a historical site of commemoration of the past…one should not hinder the Arabs from behaving there as they now do."[8] The Israeli defense minister believed that Islam must be allowed to express its religious sovereignty—as opposed to national sovereignty—over the mount; that the Arab-Israeli conflict must be kept on the territorial-national level; and that the potential for a conflict between the Jewish religion and the Muslim religion must be removed. In granting Jews the right to visit the mount, Dayan sought to placate the Jewish demands for worship and sovereignty there. In giving religious sovereignty over the mount to the Muslims, he believed he was defusing the site as a center of Palestinian nationalism.[9]

The basic elements of the status quo that Dayan designed on the Temple Mount have remained the same up to the present. Despite countless attempts by Jews to pray on the mount, the state has upheld the prohibition on Jewish prayer there. According to the Protection of Holy Places Law (1967), the religious affairs minister is indeed authorized to exercise his power and lay down regulations for Jewish and Muslim prayer on the mount; but those who have held this post have avoided doing so, conforming with the governmental decree. The Supreme Court as well, to which Jews have appealed numerous times to change this policy and allow Jews to pray at their holiest of places, has backed the government's policy for considerations of "maintaining order and public security." The court has determined that the right to pray is not enforceable without regulations, and that implementing the right without such regulations would pose a grave danger to public peace.[10] In its ruling in the case of *The Temple Mount Faithful*[11] *v. Tzahi Hanegbi* (the internal security minister at the time),[12] the court clarified that

> every Jew has the right to ascend the Temple Mount, to pray on it, and to commune with his Creator. That is part of the freedom of religious worship; that is part of the freedom of expression. At the same time, this right, like other basic rights, is not an absolute right, and in a place at which the likelihood of damage to the public peace and even to human life is almost certain—this can justify limiting the freedom of religious worship and also limiting the freedom of expression.[13]

June 1967. Defense Minister Moshe Dayan announces to the Wakf and the heads of the Supreme Muslim Council that they will be able to administer the compound themselves, while the Jews will be able to visit but not pray there. (courtesy of Schocken Books)

Even the rabbinical establishment has long assented to this policy de facto for its own reasons, which are rooted in Halakhah (Jewish religious law). The prohibition on Jews entering the Temple Mount is anchored in the Halakhic status of Jews in our times, who are regarded as "defiled by contact with the dead."[14] At present, unlike in ancient times, there is no possibility of being purified from this defilement. Not all the rabbis have agreed with this prohibition, and recent years have seen a great increase in the number of rabbis who have changed their stance and permitted Jews to enter the mount. At the same time, the Israeli Chief Rabbinate, which is the decisive institutional actor when it comes to Halakhah, has so far stuck to its position that Jews may not enter the mount.[15] Almost all the adjudicators in the haredi (ultra-Orthodox) world think the same,[16] and so do many of the leading religious-Zionist adjudicators.

An even wider consensus is embodied in the almost comprehensive Halakhic ruling that it is forbidden at present to build the Third Temple, for which Jews yearn in their prayers. This opinion is common to both rabbis who now permit entry to the Temple Mount and those who prohibit it. The rabbis categorically forbid building the Temple, whether the proposal entails building it in place of the mosques or within the mount compound but without harming them. The possibility of building the Temple is negated for several reasons; the main ones are:

1. The view that building the Temple will be allowed only with the coming of the Messiah.
2. Many believe that the Third Temple will not be built in human times but will descend, complete, from the heavens.
3. A good many more view the contemporary generation as lacking a sufficient level of spirituality, purity, and maturity to be worthy of the Temple.
4. The Halakhic obstacle to the entry of Jews to the mount, and the absence of the "red heifer," whose ash, according to Jewish sources, served in ancient times to purify Jews defiled by death.
5. The fear of an interreligious clash between Islam and Judaism involving harm to Jews and Jewish religious targets all over the world.

Seemingly, the logic of many Halakhic adjudicators concerning the Temple Mount over the years was summed up by the former deputy president of the Israel Supreme Court, Menachem Elon, in his ruling on *The Temple Mount Faithful v. the Attorney-General*. Elon explained that "this special attitude in the world of Judaism, that the more sacred the place or the issue is, there is a special duty not to draw near to it or enter it, does not entail distancing or avoidance but, rather, nearness and veneration." He also quoted statements in this spirit by Rabbi Avraham Yitzchak Hacohen Kook, who discussed the issue of the Temple and the Temple Mount at length.[17] Similar words were written more recently by Rabbi Shlomo Aviner, head of the Ateret Cohanim yeshiva, in his book *Shalhevetya*: "Our ownership and our belonging are revealed in the fact that we do not approach this place, and our national genius is evident in the fact that we show the whole world that: there is a place that we do not enter...the distance does not separate. On the contrary—it connects."[18]

For his part, Rabbi Yuval Sherlo, head of the *hesder* (combining military service and religious study) yeshiva in Petah Tikva and one of the leading rabbis of religious Zionism, takes a more complex position. Like hundreds of other Zionist rabbis, Sherlo advocates

Jewish prayer on the Temple Mount[19] but does not countenance harming the mosques. He recognizes the value of the mount and is not prepared to relinquish the Jewish connection to it, while also appreciating the obstacles to fully realizing that connection. Sherlo is in favor of studying the issues of holiness and the Temple, and of "internalizing the constant feeling that something is lacking for us," but he also emphasizes that "the building of the Temple begins at a different place"—from the standpoint of "I will build a Temple in my heart, a place for doing justice, charity, morality, and law between a man and his fellow and amending the world and society."[20]

Over the years the State of Israel has adhered—mainly with the help of its security mechanisms, the Shin Bet (Israel Security Agency) and the police—to Dayan's status quo. Furthermore, Israel initiated or accepted two major changes on the Temple Mount, to the benefit of the Muslim side.

First, notwithstanding Dayan's original decision, for many years the police have not allowed free entry by Jews to the Temple Mount, even for mere visits. The police restrict the number of Jews, particularly religious Jews, who can enter. Only a few dozen religious Jews are allowed to be there at once, and they are shadowed by Wakf guards and policemen who keep an eye on them, check their belongings to make sure they have not "smuggled" onto the mount a *tallit* (prayer shawl), *tefillin* (phylacteries), or prayer book, while warily ascertaining that their lips are not moving in prayer.[21] Only after such a contingent of religious Jews has left is another group of a few dozen allowed to enter. The hours of entry for Jews to the mount are also restricted and meager, and in times of riots and tensions the site is closed to them altogether.[22]

Second, in the mid-1990s two large underground recesses on the Temple Mount were modified, greatly expanding the area available for Muslim prayer: the underground recess at the southeastern corner of the mount, which is called Solomon's Stables (for the Muslims, the Al-Marwani Mosque), and the recess under the Al-Aksa Mosque, which is called Ancient Al-Aksa.

The archeological management of the Temple Mount is also carried out under difficult limitations. These stem from the Wakf's position that it is the sovereign, the ruler, and the decision-maker for the site. The State of Israel shows deference toward this position even though officially it does not agree with it. For example, there were years in which archeological management was not permitted at all. Quite often, rehabilitation, renovation, and building work on the mount is performed (in coordination with the Israeli government) by foreign governments and bodies, such as Jordan or Egypt, while the State of Israel "tiptoes" around these projects. In the 1994 peace treaty with Jordan, the Israeli government also recognized Jordan's future senior status regarding the Muslim holy places in Jerusalem including the mount (Al-Haram al-Sharif), at such time as peace treaties and final status agreements will be signed with the rest of the Arab world.

The fact that the official and actual policy of the State of Israel leaves the management of the Temple Mount in the hands of the Muslim Wakf is not recognized in the Muslim world today.

The fact that the official and actual policy of the State of Israel, as embodied in decisions of the Chief Rabbinical Council, the government, and the Supreme Court, leaves the management of the Temple Mount in the hands of the Muslim Wakf is not recognized in the Muslim world today. On the contrary, Palestinian and Muslim elements portray the activities of nongovernmental and nonmainstream Jewish elements, some of them extreme and marginal, who seek an immediate renewal of Temple worship and even the destruction of the mosques, as reflecting the official and actual position of the State of Israel.[23]

The reality, of course, is different. The State of Israel acts to foil such plans. Over the years extreme, nonofficial Jewish elements have tried to damage the Temple Mount and its mosques, and Muslim extremists have made use of it for purposes of terror and incitement. These attempts have been thwarted by the iron hand of the Israeli security authorities: the police, the Shin Bet, and the Mossad. It is only this overall security responsibility for the site that the State of Israel has maintained exclusively.[24] Nevertheless, all keys to the gates of the Temple Mount compound, except for the Mughrabi Gate (on its western side), are exclusively in the hands of the Wakf. Only the keys to the Mughrabi Gate are held jointly by the Wakf and Israel, with each side having a copy.

Israel has also passed the Protection of Holy Places Law. It stipulates that these places will be protected against desecration and any other harm, and against anything that could detract from the different religions' freedom of access to these places, or injure feelings connected to them. The punishments for transgressors are severe: seven years in prison for whoever desecrates a holy place, five years in prison for "whosoever does anything likely to violate the freedom of access of the members of the different religions to the places sacred to them or their feelings with regard to those places."[25]

Taking all this into account, the claim that the state and its institutions have formulated a plot to destroy the Temple Mount mosques, and establish the Third Temple in their stead, is absurd and invalid. The State of Israel has indeed adhered to the Jewish heritage, honors Jewish history, and sees itself as committed to its ancient roots, a context in which the Temple Mount and the Temple are central. Regarding the mount, however, this involves an ideological and spiritual heritage, not a practical one; a profound bond and commitment, but only on the level of consciousness. At the same time, the State of Israel does just about everything, in both its statements and its actions, to make clear that it has no intentions of building the Third Temple or destroying the Temple Mount mosques. All this has in no way prevented the many-faceted "Al-Aksa is in danger" libel from developing and taking hold of the imaginations and hearts of tens of millions of Muslims.

Advocate of the "Al-Aksa Is in Danger" Libel: Grand Mufti Haj Amin al-Husseini

The mufti, Haj Amin al-Husseini, father of the "Al-Aksa is in danger" libel. (Government Press Office)

The birthfather of the "Al-Aksa is in danger" libel, the first in the new era to claim that the Jews were scheming to destroy the Al-Aksa Mosque and build the Third Temple in its place, was Grand Mufti Haj Amin al-Husseini.[1] He lived for three-quarters of a century, until 1974, and had a particular impact on Palestine in the first half of the twentieth century. His life and teachings, however, are still relevant today. Regarding the Temple Mount mosques and the "Al-Aksa is in danger" libel, his successors, including the chairman of Fatah and the Palestinian Authority, Yasser Arafat, and the current head of the northern branch of the Israeli Islamic Movement, Raed Salah, have carried his torch.

Husseini was born in Jerusalem at the end of the nineteenth century. He was the son of the mufti of Jerusalem at that time, Taher al-Husseini, known as one of the fervent opponents of Zionism. The Jerusalemite Husseini family claims to be descended from Hussein, son of the caliph Ali, and his wife Fatima, daughter of the Prophet Muhammad. Amin al-Husseini was educated in Jerusalem. At the age of seventeen he went to study at the Islamic university of Al-Azhar in Cairo, where he spent two years. He then traveled to Mecca for the first time and won the title of Haj. When World War I broke out he was enlisted into the Ottoman army, but two years later he came down with dysentery and returned to Jerusalem. He was appointed to his first public post in 1918, in the office of the British military governor of Jerusalem. A year later Husseini was awarded a junior position in the British military administration in Damascus. There he began making contact with the nationalist circles in the court of Emir Feisal bin Hussein, and he took part in bringing representatives of the "Palestine region" to the Pan-Syrian Congress held in July 1919. At that point he was already combining educational work, political activity, and religious activity. When he returned from Damascus, Husseini joined one of the Christian-Muslim societies that were then active in Palestine. The common denominator of all of these organizations was fierce opposition to Zionism and Jewish immigration along with a Syrian orientation.

Grand Mufti Haj Amin al-Husseini meeting Adolf Hitler in 1940. (Government Press Office)

The first significant event in which Husseini played a role was a particularly violent one. In April 1920, at the end of the Nebi Musa holiday[2] as thousands of Muslims returned in a procession from Nebi Musa to Jerusalem, Husseini fired up the crowd. The procession deteriorated into severe violence and on the way five Jews were murdered and 211 injured.[3] Leading the procession itself was Husseini's stepbrother, Mufti Kamel al-Husseini, who, in contrast to Amin, tried (unsuccessfully) to subdue the passions. The British issued an arrest warrant for Amin al-Husseini, who fled across the Jordan and from there to Damascus. In his absence he was given a military sentence of ten years' imprisonment. Five months later, when Sir Herbert Samuel assumed the post of high commissioner, the exiled Haj Amin was granted a pardon.

When Husseini returned to Jerusalem he was received by the city's Arabs as a hero, one who had dared rebel against the British and fight against the Jews. Upon the death of his stepbrother, Mufti Kamel al-Husseini, Haj Amin competed over the succession. At first he lost to contenders with higher Muslim religious education than his own, but he and his family refused to give in. They mounted heavy pressure, including public announcements and protests, until finally the appointment went to Haj Amin when he was just twenty-six years old. Two years later, when the Supreme Muslim Council was established, he was elected to lead it.

Now that he held both of the senior religious positions, Husseini launched the enterprise of renovating the Dome of the Rock and the Al-Aksa Mosque on the Temple Mount. This further boosted his power and popularity among Muslims both locally and globally.

The two mosques had indeed fallen into neglect and disrepair with renovation urgently needed, but this task, which Husseini made sure would attract plenty of publicity, was for him a lever to further goals: exalted personal status in the Muslim world, harnessing the Muslim countries to the national struggle of the Palestinians, and drawing the gazes of millions of Muslims the world over to the holy places of Islam in Jerusalem and on the Temple Mount.[4]

By the end of 1924 about ninety thousand pounds sterling had been collected, and to further impress the target audience and recruit still more funds, Husseini's emissaries carried "proofs" of the danger the Jews posed to the Temple Mount mosques. These were apparently leaflets for soliciting contributions to Jewish Torah institutions in Jerusalem (for example, the Torah of Life Yeshiva), and propaganda materials of various Zionist groups, which included drawings of the Al-Aksa Mosque or the Dome of the Rock adorned with Jewish symbols, primarily Stars of David.[5] These propaganda materials helped directors of the Jewish institutions in Palestine mobilize funds from Jewish donors abroad. In vain did Yishuv leaders explain that these materials were solely for fundraising, as had already been the practice for many decades. Another issue was the traditional Jewish adornment known as the Mizrach (East), which included a picture of the Temple Mount and its mosques and had been hung in numerous Jewish homes in Palestine and abroad for hundreds of years to mark Jerusalem as the direction of prayer. Husseini and his comrades, however, used the Mizrach to incite against the Jews and the Zionist movement, and kept claiming that the Jews were plotting to destroy the mosques and build the Temple in their stead.[6] Husseini himself asserted that "Zionism is both a religious and a political Jewish idea," and that among its goals were the "rebuilding of the Temple that is called Solomon's Temple in place of the blessed Al-Aksa Mosque and the conducting of religious worship in it."[7]

When Husseini took on the task of renovating the Temple Mount mosques, it was clear how severely they had been neglected. The heritage of the Ottomans, when it came to the maintenance of the two Muslim prayer houses on the mount, was abject. Since the defeat of the Crusaders and the changes Saladin had carried out at the site, over seven hundred years had passed. The earthquake that struck Jerusalem in 1927 had also done its damage. Husseini ordered the destruction of all of the lengthwise walls and arcades on the eastern side of the Al-Aksa Mosque. The old columns were removed, with white marble columns brought from Italy to replace them. The ceilings were reconstructed in an ancient Muslim style, and dozens of rugs, a gift of the king of Morocco, were spread throughout most of the mosque. The upkeep of Al-Haram al-Sharif improved greatly, and within its confines a museum of the history of Islam and a library of religious materials were established.[8]

Husseini went in two directions at once. With one hand he renovated the mosques and enhanced their status, along with his own. With the other hand he constantly dealt in incitement and outright lies against the Jews. Husseini exploited the Jews' struggle for their right to pray at the Western Wall, and for better conditions in its narrow prayer plaza, to whip up animosity against them and accuse them of much more ambitious aims: the destruction of the mosques and the building of the Third Temple in their stead.

Husseini exploited the Jews' struggle for their right to pray at the Western Wall to whip up animosity against them and accuse them of much more ambitious aims: the destruction of the mosques and the building of the Third Temple in their stead.

It is common knowledge that Jews have prayed at the foot of the Western Wall of the Temple Mount compound for hundreds of years. Up to the present they view the wall as the last remnant of the Temple, even if historically speaking it is a wall of the compound as a whole and not of the Temple itself, which was a structure within the compound. Against this backdrop Jews also tried to acquire the narrow prayer plaza at the foot of the wall.[9] It became widely known as "the Jewish Wall of Tears," which tells much about whom it was associated with. Indeed, Jews have visited and prayed at the Western Wall since at least the twelfth century.[10] It was most likely in the sixteenth century that regular prayer began in the current area of the plaza, and the Western Wall gained its status as the second holiest place for Jews, after the mount itself. In that century the Ottoman sultan Suleiman the Lawgiver (also known as "the Magnificent") also recognized its status, and granted the Jews a *firman* (authorization) that acknowledged their right to pray at the spot.[11]

Before describing the developments that led to intensified conflict over the Western Wall and the outbreak of the 1929 riots, it is worth considering a different process: *how*

the holiness that Muslims attributed to two of the walls of the Temple Mount somehow migrated to the Western Wall. Sura 17:1 of the Koran tells of the Night Journey, in which the Prophet Muhammad was brought from the Holy Mosque (apparently in Mecca) to the Farthest Mosque, whose identity is unknown. Some Muslim oral traditions, however, identified the Farthest Mosque with the Temple Mount in Jerusalem. These traditions say Muhammad came to Jerusalem on the back of a wondrous winged creature called Al-Buraq, and, when he reached the mount, tethered the animal and then ascended from the holy Rock of the mount to the heavens.

388 Jews' Wailing Place. Klagemauer Le Mur de Pleurs.

Dr. Shmuel Berkovitz, a scholar of the holy places in the Land of Israel, found that until the eleventh century, Muslim scholars disagreed as to the location of the tethering of Muhammad's steed and pointed to different places on Al-Haram al-Sharif.[12] Some said the place of Muhammad's entry to Haram and the tethering of Al-Buraq was the Eastern Wall. Others said it was the Southern Wall, but no one at all looked to the Western Wall as the place where Al-Buraq was tethered. In the seventeenth century, it was common to identify a spot close to the southwestern corner of the mount as the site of the tethering. The archeologist Meir Ben-Dov believes that the Muslim traditions identifying the place as the Western Wall began at the end of the nineteenth century,[13] just when the wall was gradually becoming a symbol of the renewed Jewish settlement in the Land of Israel.[14]

Apparently not by coincidence, it was soon after, at the beginning of the twentieth century, that the Jews began bringing to the prayer plaza various furnishings and ritual articles: chairs, benches, tables, and Torah volumes, while also renewing the attempts to acquire the plaza, which was owned by the Wakf. Seemingly, then, the identification of the Western Wall as the site of the tethering of Al-Buraq came as a Muslim religio-political reaction to what the Muslims called "the Jewish takeover of the Western Wall." In this period the Muslims also began pointing to the underground room that is beneath the Al-Buraq Mosque, on the inner side of the Western Wall, as the place where Muhammad tethered Al-Buraq, and to the Berkeley Gate, which is concealed under the Mughrabi Gate, as the one through which Muhammad entered the sacred compound.

When a *mechitsa* (partition) was put up at the Western Wall in September 1928, so as to separate between men and women in prayer as practiced in Orthodox Judaism, and when benches for sitting were also brought to the prayer plaza as well as ritual objects, the Supreme Muslim Council convened and called on Muslims to oppose "the Jews' ambitions to take over the holy places of Islam."

All the explanations of the Jewish side that it had no intentions to take over the Muslim holy places were to no avail. In November 1928, the National Committee of the Jews of the Land of Israel published an open letter to the Arabs that stated, among other things:

> We hereby announce, honestly and sincerely, that no one from Israel has any intention of infringing the rights of Muslims to the places that are holy to them. However, our Arab brothers must also recognize the rights that Israel has in this land, to our own places....Any attempt to describe the desire of the Jews to pray at this holy place, the Western Wall plaza, in peace, with respect and without restriction, as the creation of a strategic base for an attack on the mosques of the Muslims, is nothing but the fruit of a fevered imagination or a malicious libel. The aim of this libel is to sow tumult and confusion in hearts and arouse animosity and conflict between different peoples.[15]

Not only did this announcement not work, but the Muslim Council further upped the ante. They forged an opening in the southern part of the Western Wall plaza so as to change the Jews' place of prayer into a passageway for both man and beast, and used various stratagems to further disrupt the Jews' worship. This campaign was orchestrated by the mufti Haj Amin. Some of the restrooms of homes alongside the prayer plaza were actually adjacent to the wall,[16] and from time to time the Muslims would dump feces and garbage in the narrow plaza. In the spring of 1929, the Muslims in those residences abutting the plaza began conducting noisy ceremonies that included shouts, dances, and songs to the sounds of cymbals and drums. For the first time the ceremony known as Dikar was held in that locale, and for the first time it was timed for the hour when Jewish worshippers were there.[17]

At the beginning of August 1929, Arabs attacked and injured Jews who had come to pray at the Western Wall.[18] On August 15, the night of the Jewish holiday of Tisha B'Av, the Betar movement and the Jewish community in the country brought tens of thousands in an impressive march to the Western Wall. The Arab protest, however, rose to a new pitch, with ceaseless harassment of the Jewish worshippers at the spot and an incitement campaign against the Jews' supposed aim to take over the Temple Mount and its mosques. This ongoing incitement, in which Husseini played a central role, eventually erupted in large-scale pogroms against Jews, which came to be known as the "1929 riots." A week after the Tisha B'Av march, the signal came from Al-Aksa. Masses of *fellahin* from the surrounding villages assembled, bearing clubs and knives. The inflamed Arab mass attacked Jewish neighborhoods in Jerusalem, and from there the pogroms spread to Jewish agricultural settlements such as Motza, Be'er Tuvia, and Hulda, Jewish urban concentrations such as Haifa and Tel Aviv, and the mixed cities of Hebron and Safed. The mayhem went on for a week. One hundred and thirty-three Jews, mostly in Safed and Hebron, were butchered. Three hundred and thirty-nine Jews were injured. Eight Jewish settlements had to be abandoned, and the events came to be etched as a terrible calamity in the collective memory of the Jews of Israel.[19]

The "Al-Aksa is in danger" libel and its use by the mufti led to pogroms against Jews in Israel. In the photo: Jews of the Old City being evacuated by British soldiers, 1936. (Erik Matson, Government Press Office)

The historian Prof. Yehoshua Porat later maintained that the renovation of the mosques, and subsequent disruptions at the Western Wall, were the crowning glory of Haj Amin al-Husseini's activities. "Toward 1929 the mosques on the Temple Mount became a symbol of the struggle against Zionism. This was a tangible symbol, clear and understood to all, which replaced abstract national slogans of self-definition. Under this approach, the problem of the Land of Israel began to exceed the narrow borders of the land and became a pan-Arab and pan-Islamic problem."[20] In other words, Husseini's behavior did not stem from religious faith alone. He concocted the "Al-Aksa is in danger" libel as part of the building of the Palestinian national ethos, which in those days was still in its earliest stage. He identified the points of ostensible overlap and competition over the holy places of the two religions, emphasized them, and used them as fuel for the fire. The higher its flames rose, the better his purposes were served.

Zvi Elpeleg, a scholar of Husseini who has studied his articles and other writings, found that the sources Haj Amin used supposedly to prove his claims of a Jewish plot were fatally flawed. Elpeleg discovered a selective choice of quotations and a lifting of them from their context.[21]

Elpeleg pointed, for example, to statements by the mufti that were drawn from the *Encyclopaedia Britannica*. From there the mufti took the sentence: "The Jews aspire... to rebuild the Temple and reestablish the Kingdom of David in Jerusalem, headed by a prince from the House of David,"[22] and made a distorted use of it. Husseini was basing himself on the entry on "Zionism" in the encyclopedia's 1926 edition. He did not inform his readers that the words were written in connection to the Prophets, in the context of a vision of the End of Days and the coming of the Messiah. He also did not bother explaining that, while the history of the Jewish people in the Land of Israel and the existence of the Temple indeed form the background of Zionism, the late-nineteenth-century heralds of this Jewish national movement were patently secular individuals. The Zionist movement was political in its goals and methods, and its leaders sought to find a political and territorial solution for the Jews. For them the building of the Temple was not part of that solution. The same *Encyclopaedia Britannica* article noted that Theodor Herzl, who foresaw the Jewish state, at first was prepared to solve the Jewish problem in an autonomous political framework anywhere in the world, not necessarily in the Land of Israel. That did not stop Husseini from charging Zionism with "schemes" to destroy the mosques and build the Temple.

The mufti distorted other "quotes" as well, which he attributed to Ben-Gurion. The latter wrote that "indeed the religious Jews believe...that the Temple will be rebuilt, but this will be done only after the coming of the Messiah. This is a religious belief, and the believers are certain that this will happen through a divine miracle, and not through nature....And no Jew contemplates for a moment touching the holy places of other peoples."[23] Husseini was well aware that the Jews sought nothing more than to exercise their right to pray at the Western Wall. Yet, in his doctored version, this meant the Jews aimed to take over the mosques and do them harm.

Elpeleg, who translated and annotated the mufti's articles, found that this issue "continued to serve the mufti's propaganda machine in later periods as well and basically until the end of his life." Nevertheless, if in the 1920s the mosques sacred to Islam in Jerusalem and the Western Wall stood at the center of the Jewish-Arab conflict, in the 1930s and 1940s, as the struggle over the land's political future intensified, the holy places lost their centrality. Elpeleg observes that by 1967 the issue had almost disappeared from the Palestinians' claims.[24]

Once the mufti's status began to decline, the mask was removed from his face. His flight from Palestine and cooperation with the Nazis bear dramatic witness to his true path, of which the "Al-Aksa is in danger" libel was part and parcel. In the Muslim Congress of 1931, Haj Amin's status was still strong and, despite the many rivalries within the Palestinian camp, no one questioned his supremacy. For five years Husseini succeeded to play a double game—a seemingly moderate dialogue partner for the Mandate authorities, and yet, toward his own people, a chauvinist and firebrand. The British then discovered, however, that he was receiving assistance—funds, weapons,

The Iron Gate, 1938. During the Great Arab Revolt the Temple Mount became a focal point of Muslim incitement and the British closed its gates for several months. (Erik Matson, Government Press Office)

and guidance in waging the revolt that he launched in 1936—from Mussolini's Italy and Hitler's Germany. With that their tolerance ran out, and they sent the police to arrest him. Husseini, however, managed to escape to Jaffa dressed as a woman, and from there made it in a boat to Lebanon,[25] where he was arrested by the French coast guard. He was given refuge there but his movement was restricted.[26]

Now he no longer had to hide his real commitments. He acted against France in Syria and against the British in Iraq, and in the World War II years he found a haven in Germany, serving as an adviser to those carrying out the policy of annihilating the Jews of Europe. In Yugoslavia, Husseini set up a Muslim SS division.[27] Documents that surfaced over the years shed new light on the depth of his loathing for Jews. He called Adolf Eichmann "the greatest friend of the Arabs."[28] On November 28, 1941, he met with Hitler and learned that he had "decided to find a solution to the Jewish problem, in stages, step after step, without pause."[29] On another opportunity he looked into a possibility to bomb Tel Aviv,[30] and in 1942 he signed a letter together with Iraqi prime minister Rashid Ali al-Kilani that expressed support for Germany and its aim of obliterating the Jewish home in Palestine.[31] During his stay in Germany he also gave speeches on Radio Berlin and said: "Kill the Jews wherever you find them. This finds grace in the eyes of God, history and religion."[32]

In 1970, the journalist Haviv Canaan disclosed that the mufti had been planning to build crematoriums for Jews in Samaria's Dotan Valley. Canaan based his words on the testimony of Faiz Bei Adrisi, senior Arab officer in the Mandate police and commander of the village subdistrict of the Jerusalem district, who told him that Haj Amin aimed to enter Jerusalem at the head of his subordinates, the soldiers of the Arab Legion that was organized in the framework of the German army. His great plan was to build in the Dotan Valley, near Nablus, giant crematoriums of the Auschwitz kind, to which the Jews of the Land of Israel as well as the Jews of Iraq, Egypt, Yemen, Syria, Lebanon, and even North Africa would be brought, so as to annihilate them with the methods used by the SS in the death camps of Europe.[33]

In the last days of the war, Husseini was captured by French forces on German soil and put in Fontainebleau Prison near Paris. He was declared a war criminal; the Arab states, which demanded his release, viewed him as a national hero. A few weeks later Husseini was snatched from the prison, and after the war he surfaced in Switzerland and went to live in Egypt.

In 1954, the mufti Haj Amin briefly returned to the "Al-Aksa is in danger" allegation, apparently in the context of talks held at that time on the resettlement of Palestinian refugees in Arab countries and feelers for a final agreement between Arab states and Israel. This, in any case, was to be his swansong on the issue. In 1966, a year before Israel unified the two parts of Jerusalem, Husseini managed to visit the Kingdom of Jordan. The establishment of the PLO drew him closer to his historical rivals from the Hashemite royal family. According to one assessment, Husseini hoped to be the leader of the autonomy that Jordan's King Hussein envisaged for the West Bank; in 1974, however, Husseini died in Beirut. His request was to be buried in Jerusalem, but the State of Israel did not allow it.

The Muslims Rewrite the History of Jerusalem

From the moment Jerusalem was unified in June 1967 and its eastern part came under Israeli rule, the Palestinians and the Arabs began to portray Al-Haram al-Sharif as "Al-Aksa that has fallen prisoner to the Jews," while the mount rose to the status of Islamic holiness.[1] So long as a Muslim sovereign ruled in Jerusalem, the religious leadership of the Arabs of Palestine, from their seat on the Temple Mount, concentrated on religious practice, with very little role for political matters in their activities. But Jerusalem's conquest by non-Muslim rulers, whether Christian Crusaders at the beginning of the second millennium or Jews at the end of that millennium, catapulted Jerusalem from a religious symbol of secondary importance to a religious-national symbol of the first order.[2]

The historian and Middle East scholar Prof. Emmanuel Sivan notes in his book *Arab Political Myths* that in the early period of Islam, no special sanctity was attributed to Jerusalem. As he observes:

> The extent to which Islam at its inception did not accord importance to Jerusalem can be proved by the fact that Jerusalem was one of the last cities to be conquered at the time of the invasion of Syria, after the death of Muhammad, and that its conquest is associated with the name of a junior commander and not – as later legends claim – with the name of the revered Caliph Omar himself. Furthermore, the city did not even become the capital of the new province of Palestine. Its new lords called it Ayela, an Arabic version of the Roman name Aelia Capitolina. Nor was the city the municipal seat of Palestine. That was initially Caesarea and subsequently Ramle.[3]

Praying at the Al-Aksa Mosque, July 1967. Worship there was immediately renewed with the end of the Six-Day War. (Fritz Cohen, Government Press Office)

Sivan points out that while the sacredness of Jerusalem was a widespread notion at the end of the seventh century, mainly because of factors on the popular level, its revival in the mid-twelfth century was instigated from above by ruling circles—initially by Zengi, the Turkish emir of the state of Mosul-Halav, who conquered the Crusader principality of Odessa in northern Syria. This emir was the first ruler of his time to declare a *jihad* aimed at obliterating the entire Crusader presence in the East. The liberation of Jerusalem was made a supreme objective of the campaign and the keynote of its propagandizing. Zengi's son, Nur ad-Din, continued in this path, and one of his court poets wrote in one of his poems:

> The infidel rulers must hand over [to Zengi] not only
> Odessa but also the rest of their lands.
> All this land is his.
> If the conquest of Odessa is the sea, then Jerusalem,
> And the Crusader Kingdom within it, is its shore.[4]

In the days of Saladin this push further intensified, and the Dome of the Rock was described as "rejoicing at the news that the Koran, which she has been lacking, is to return."[5] In the sultan's missive that proclaimed to all the princes of Islam the victory in the Battle of Hattin (July 4, 1187), he promised to immediately impose a siege on Jerusalem: "the darkness of heresy has so long enfolded her, and very soon the dawn of redemption will shine on her."

As we have seen, a similar phenomenon occurred after 1967, but this time it was brought about by "Jewish infidels" instead of "Crusader infidels." Under the rule of the Jordanian monarchy, Jerusalem's status had drastically declined.[6] Now, in the wake of the Six-Day War, the city suddenly rebounded in holiness and political importance. Poems and yearnings for Muslim Jerusalem were published in the Arab world, and almost every self-respecting Arab ruler set up a special committee on Jerusalem and the Temple Mount.[7] Over the years, military units, camps, schools, clubs, refugee camps in the West Bank, conferences, conventions, and committees were given the name Al-Aksa.

Jerusalem's unification under Israeli sovereignty in 1967 also immediately piqued Arab rulers' interest in the city in general and in Al-Haram al-Sharif with its pair of sacred shrines in particular. Arab leaders made sure to weave into their speeches words of longing for the Temple Mount mosques, "which are being defiled by the Jews," and to raise generous contributions for the renovation and maintenance of the compound. Any involvement, even if symbolic, with the sacred place was portrayed as assistance and devotion to the national struggle for liberation of the occupied lands.[8]

From the standpoint of the Arab countries, making the connection with the Temple Mount was an act of solidarity in the battle against Israel and proof of unreserved loyalty to the national struggle of the Palestinians. In the years immediately after the Six-Day War, hundreds of organizations, councils, and committees on Jerusalem and Al-Aksa popped up in the Arab countries like mushrooms after rain, and many of these continued to exist for many years thereafter.

For tens of millions of residents of Arab countries, Islam and their Arab nationalism are interlinked. They do not necessarily distinguish between one and the other. Allegiance to Islam is often proof of allegiance to the national struggle. While the use of religious symbols for political and national purposes is not an invention of Islam, it is hard to give the flavor of the Arab states' ongoing struggle against Israel without the religious symbols that have sustained it, and all the more powerfully after the Six-Day War and Israeli rule over Jerusalem and the Temple Mount.

Even the name of Fatah, for many years the military wing of the PLO, manifests the Muslim ethos. In Arabic the acronym for Fatah is the initials in reverse of the Movement for the Liberation of Palestine, representing Sura 48 or "Sura al-Fatah" of the Koran, which glorifies the conquest of Mecca by Muhammad's army and extols the victory of Islam through holy war—*jihad*. Hundreds of newspapers and journals throughout the Arab world, of various ideological hues and sharply differing political slants, continue to feature a photo of the Dome of the Rock on the front page. Al-Aksa became a trademark and a national symbol. Glorifying in it attested to one's fealty to the Islamic holy places of Jerusalem and effectively shielded one against possible accusations of insufficient nationalism by extreme Palestinians. The terror gangs of Fatah are called the Al-Aksa Brigades. The Palestinian Authority's police company in Jericho, and the police camp there, are called the Al-Aksa Company and the Al-Aksa Camp. The Second Intifada that erupted in 2000 was called the Al-Aksa Intifada, and the Arab summit that convened after it broke out was called the Al-Aksa summit.[9] Even Christian Arabs view the Al-Aksa Mosque compound as a national symbol.[10]

After the war Jerusalem sprang forth in new colors in Muslim literature and poetry as well. Particularly successful was a song by the late, beloved songstress Oum Kalthoum, "The Three Holy Cities." In its third stanza dealing with Jerusalem, Oum Kalthoum as well sowed the seeds of the "Al-Aksa is in danger" libel, which in the years to come would take on such profound dimensions:

> From the place from which Muhammad ascended at night to the heavens,
> From Jerusalem the pure and clear,
> I hear...a cry for help
> I bear witness that the enemies burned
> The holiest place of all
> And paced on it in arrogance
> I hear the sad stones
> Lamenting in the darkness of night:
> Alas for Jerusalem captured by the aggressor.[11]

A short time after the Six-Day War, the Muslims reverted to the Temple Mount's original name in Arabic. Instead of calling it Al-Haram al-Sharif, they began using the name that is mentioned in the Koran: Al-Masjid al-Aksa (the Farthest Mosque). This made it easier to confer a sacred status, similar to a mosque, on the Temple Mount as a whole, while relating accordingly to any Jewish presence on any part of the mount. From this point onward the view of the entire mount and its walls, and not only the mosques, as a holy place also shaped attitudes toward activity by the Israeli security forces on the mount, visits by Jews there, attempts by Jews to pray there, and indeed toward any Israeli connection to the compound and its walls.[12] From the Muslim standpoint, Jewish rule itself is what contaminates and desecrates the Muslimness of Jerusalem, and is fundamentally illegitimate.

In 1967, forty-six years after its creation by Haj Amin al-Husseini and sixteen years after the Jordanian authorities dismantled it, the Supreme Muslim Council was reconstituted, this time under the stewardship of the leader of the revolt against Jewish rule, Sheikh al-Sayach, who was elected as its head. In his statements and mode of leadership Al-Sayach, whom Israel eventually expelled to Jordan, was reminiscent of the mufti Amin al-Husseini. He too obtained his religious education at Al-Azhar University in Cairo and then returned to Jerusalem. The most important chapter of his life was his work with Husseini himself. At the end of the 1930s, al-Sayach was put in prison for his insurrectionary activity against Great Britain under Haj Amin's direction. The latter ramped up the status of the two mosques on the Temple Mount and, with al-Sayach's help, transformed them from a religious symbol to a national one of struggle against the renascent Zionist movement. "Religion, education and politics," the sheikh would say to his close associates, "descended bundled together from the heavens. In this path went Muhammad, and in this path I too will proceed."[13]

The events of August 1967 augmented the religious dimension of the Arab revolt that spread through eastern Jerusalem. The attempts by IDF Chief Rabbi Shlomo Goren to conduct Jewish prayers on the Temple Mount, which were obstructed by the government, brought the Muslim religious leaders, headed by al-Sayach, to publish on August 22 a ruling that set the tone—which would only gain strength in the future—for the Muslim attitude toward the Israeli sovereign presence in Jerusalem and on the mount in particular:

> Given Israel's intention to widen the Western Wall plaza, the prayer sessions of Brigadier Goren, and the declaration of the religious affairs minister that the Temple Mount is a Jewish property, on the basis of conquest and ownership, the following points must be emphasized: the Al-Aksa Mosque is the first *kibla* [direction of prayer] and the third mosque in importance in Islam. This sanctified place comprises the entire expanse of the Temple Mount, the mosque itself, the walls that surround the plaza, the gates, the plaza, the Dome of the Rock, and all the areas adjacent to it. Whoever offends the sanctity of this site, offends

the sanctity of the mosque itself....The right of ownership of the sacred Rock... has been determined by traditions and sayings over hundreds of years in which the Muslims possessed these rights, and these rights are not open to question. They cannot be questioned either before a religious court or according to local or international law.[14]

In light of this ruling, it is worth recalling how Jerusalem came to be the third holiest place in Islam. The Koran does not mention Jerusalem by name at all. Ancient Muslim commentary vacillated on the question of the identity of Al-Aksa (the farthest, the remote), which is mentioned in the context of Muhammad's Night Journey (Koran, Sura 17). Some claimed it was a heavenly mosque, but others maintained that it was in Jerusalem. After Muhammad's flight from Mecca to Medina (the *hijra* in Arabic) in 622, he ordered his believers, for a short period of sixteen months, to turn in their prayers toward the city of Jerusalem. He thereby hoped to convince Jewish tribes in the city to convert to Islam. When this failed, the *kibla* became the Kabaa in Mecca, the birthplace of the Islamic religion, near which Muhammad had his first revelation. The term for Jerusalem in the Muslim tradition remains, however, "the first *kibla*." For hundreds of years Muslim writings and sources call the city Beit al-Mikdas (the Arabic equivalent of Beit Hamikdash, which means "the Temple" in Hebrew), but it was only in the second half of the twentieth century that this name was adopted by masses of Muslim believers.[15]

In the Muslim tradition Jerusalem was third in virtue and importance after Mecca and Medina, where Muhammad and his followers migrated and found refuge from the persecution they suffered in Mecca.[16] Concerning Mecca, Medina, and Jerusalem, the Muslim tradition states: "One prayer in Mecca is weighed against ten thousand prayers. A prayer in Medina is weighed against a thousand prayers, and a prayer in Jerusalem is weighed against five hundred prayers."[17] Pilgrimage to Mecca confers the title of Haj. Pilgrimage to Jerusalem, as to all sites that are not the Kaaba in Mecca, is accorded less value. Nevertheless, Jerusalem has a central place in the Muslim view of the End of Days. As religion scholar Prof. Zvi Verblovsky put it: "There are no direct flights from Mecca to heaven. You have to make a stop in Jerusalem."[18] According to one Muslim tradition, at the End of Days the Kaaba, the black stone in Mecca, will move to Jerusalem and be affixed there.

At the end of the seventh century, in 691, about sixty years after Jerusalem was conquered by the Arabs, the Umayyad caliph Abd al-Malik created a structure for the Dome of the Rock.[19] In the view of many, the illustrious shrine was primarily intended to commemorate Islam's victory over the existing religions; emphasize the sense of connection between Islam and Jerusalem and the Temple Mount; compete aesthetically with the glorious Christian churches; and—no less important—to develop a political-religious hub in Jerusalem that, if it did not surpass Mecca, would at least be equal to it.[20] The Al-Aksa Mosque was founded in 705 by the Umayyad caliph Al-Walid, son of the founder of the

Dome of the Rock, Abd al-Malik.[21] In the course of over 1300 years the two structures have become an inseparable pair. The Dome of the Rock preserves and exalts the intrinsically sacred Rock, and within it Muslims have engaged in individual prayer; the Al-Aksa Mosque has been a place of public prayer.[22]

In his book *The Fight for Jerusalem*, Dr. Dore Gold notes that "the Muslim theologians argued among themselves as to whether the Night Journey, and the ascent to the heavens that are attributed to Muhammad, were part of the vision—that is, some sort of spiritual experience, or an event that actually occurred." The interpretation of the event as a vision was supported by Aisha (613-678), daughter of Abu Bakr and beloved wife of Muhammad, whom many consulted in her later years about the practices and sayings of the leader.[23] The Caliph Muawiyah as well, who founded the Umayyad dynasty in Damascus in 600, regarded the story of the Night Journey as a vision.[24] The Arabic inscription from the time of the Dome of the Rock, which surrounds the central octagonal portico of the structure, above the arches, consists almost completely of an intense theological debate with Christianity,[25] but makes no mention of Muhammad's dream.

Prof. Menashe Harel observes in this context that "the Al-Aksa Mosque in Jerusalem was built sixty years after Muhammad's dream and is not mentioned in the 240 meters of Koran verses that adorn the inner walls of the Dome of the Rock," and that "the Night Journey of this mosque was mentioned for the first time in the Ottoman inscription that is on the Dome of the Rock."[26] As noted, though, other scholars maintain that "originally there was an ancient stratum of traditions that located the Al-Aksa Mosque in heaven, while a second, later stratum of traditions, which was intended to emphasize the glory of Jerusalem over Mecca, located Al-Aksa in Jerusalem."[27] In the view of these researchers, the aim of Abd al-Malik, builder of the Dome of the Rock, whose capital was Damascus, was to lessen the importance of pilgrimage to Mecca (which was under the control of his rivals, followers of the Shiite caliph Abdullah ibn al-Zubayr)[28] and to exalt Jerusalem. In any case, the view that was ultimately accepted is that Muhammad came to Jerusalem physically and also ascended from it to heaven.

Thus Jerusalem became the third place in importance in Islam. In recent years, however, new layers have been added to the old traditions, and the Muslim and Arab history of Jerusalem has been rewritten. The center of gravity is now the historical right of the Arabs to Jerusalem and Palestine, and the story is built on the claim that the Arabs ruled Jerusalem for thousands of years before the Israelites.

Muslims have promulgated a denial and negation of the Jewish-Zionist narrative—including the de-Judaization of the Temple Mount, the Western Wall, and of Jerusalem altogether—making changes in a history they upheld for centuries, documented in their own writings.

This new version of the Arab-Muslim claim is, however, inadequate, since against it already stand thousands of years of the "Jewish story." Hence the Muslims have also promulgated a denial and negation of the Jewish-Zionist narrative, including the de-Judaization of the Temple Mount, the Western Wall, and of Jerusalem altogether. The changes the Muslims have made in the history they upheld for centuries, a history that is documented in their own writings, concern first and foremost the question of the age and status of Al-Aksa. The age of the mosque has been altered as dating from the ancient Muslim era.[29] "This was part of the attempt to 'Islamize' the period that preceded Muhammad's message of Islam, and to Arabize Jerusalem and the Land of Israel. The process of Islamization and Arabization stemmed from the need to claim an Arab and Islamic historical right to the sacred land, before the Israelites were there—the ancient Jews, and the Christians."[30] To this end old traditions were enlisted that attribute the building of Al-Aksa to Abraham, to the first man, or to the time of the creation of the world.[31]

The new Muslim narrative determined, for example, that the Al-Aksa Mosque was not built around 1300 years ago—which is what modern research finds—but rather by the first man, forty years after the mosque in Mecca was built. The Jordanian Wakf minister Al-Salaam al-Abadi already claimed this in 1995. The Saudi historian Muhammad Sharab, too, asserted that Al-Aksa was built by the first man, and that God himself chose the spot and meant it to be a place of worship for believers in one God. The former mufti of Jerusalem and of the Palestinian Authority, Sheikh Akrama Sabri, also repeatedly attributed the building of the mosque in Mecca and of the Al-Aksa compound to the first man, and said it was King Solomon who renewed the building of Al-Aksa. According to Sabri, Solomon did not build the Jewish Temple but, rather, the Al-Aksa compound, which is a Muslim mosque.

In recent years spokesmen of the southern branch of the Islamic Movement have been stating that Abraham is the one who built Al-Aksa about four thousand years ago, forty years after he built the Kaaba together with his son Ishmael.[32] Thus, so as to "Islamize" the era before Muhammad's message of Islam emerged, ancient Muslim traditions are mobilized that previously were of negligible importance, and to the Al-Aksa Mosque are added more ancient origins, a great deal earlier than the year of its construction and, of course, earlier than the presence of the Israelites in the Land of Israel.[33]

Lately Muslim figures have come up with a further surprise: defining, for the first time, Al-Aksa as second—not third—in holiness, still coming after Mecca but before Medina.[34] This was done, for example, by Sheikh Kamal Rian of the southern branch of the Islamic Movement, who said that "in our faith this is the second mosque. It is holier than the mosque in Medina, and this the Jews do not grasp."[35]

Along with the upgrading of the Muslim holiness of Jerusalem and Al-Aksa, a campaign has already been waged for years, as mentioned, to deny the Jewish link to Jerusalem and Judaism's holy places. A former mufti of Jerusalem, Sheikh Saad al-Din al-Alami, was very explicit on this issue when he said that the Jews contaminate the Muslimness of Jerusalem.[36]

I was personally witness to an example of this attitude when, a few years ago, I came with some archeology students from Bar-Ilan University to the Kidron Valley in Jerusalem. The students tried to retrieve archeological relics from the piles of dirt that the Wakf had dug from the Temple Mount, which were then brought in trucks and dumped in the valley. One of the Wakf officials who saw the students started bellowing at them, and one of his statements stood out: "You have nothing to look for here just as the Crusaders had nothing to look for here! Jerusalem is Muslim!"

Although such remarks could indeed have been considered anomalous in the past, all that changed with the Camp David Conference in July 2000. There it became clear to senior Israeli officials that this claim—that Jews have no real connection to Jerusalem and the holy places—had not only been widely disseminated in Arab and Muslim communities and become a staple of Arab public discourse, but that the Palestinian leadership had adopted it as well.

Arafat himself endorsed this claim at Camp David[37] and reiterated it in slightly different form in September 2003 when he lectured to a delegation of Arab leaders from the Galilee and told them that the Jewish Temple had not been located in Jerusalem but, rather, in Yemen. "I myself," Arafat "testified," "visited Yemen and was shown the site where the Temple of Solomon existed."[38] Arafat apparently drew this theory from a book by the historian Kamal Salibi, professor emeritus of the American University in Beirut, who was appointed to direct the Royal Institute for Inter-Faith Studies in Jordan.[39] Saeb Erekat as well, who has been a Palestinian negotiator since the Madrid Conference in 1991, also cast doubt on the Jewish connection to Jerusalem during the 2000 Camp David Conference.[40]

That the senior official representatives of the Palestinian Authority embraced Temple denial, and flung it shamelessly at Jewish statesmen, is seemingly the best testimony to the assimilation of the new narrative that the Muslims have written for Jerusalem. The Israeli statesmen, who were not members of the Jewish Temple Mount movement, did not conceal their amazement and consternation when confronted with this reality.

Such sentiments are evident in a 2002 article by Yossi Alpher, a former senior Mossad member who directed the Jaffee Center for Strategic Studies at Tel Aviv University. Alpher, a secular Jew who also is not suspected of excessive closeness to the Temple Mount movement, and is known for his readiness for far-reaching compromises for peace, wrote:

Of all the declarations concerning the peace process that were voiced by Yasser Arafat and his associates in the months from Camp David (July 2000) to Taba (January 2001), none was as offensive and disturbing as the claim that there was never a Temple on the Temple Mount. Indeed, Arafat annulled the basic tenet of the Jewish faith that the Land of Israel is the historical homeland of the Jewish people. Like the majority of Jews, religious and secular, I saw in these statements an attempt to subvert our national identity.

"As a secular Jew," Alpher explained,

I feel no need to pray—not at the Western Wall and not on the Temple Mount; however, I do require a visit to the mount itself. I can accept that we will never have an opportunity to excavate and recover the relics on the mount. I, like a majority of Jews, do not seek to reestablish the Temple....But in a more profound sense, the Palestinian denial of the narrative that links the Jewish people to the Temple Mount—like the demand that Israel agree "in principle" to the right of return of the Palestinian refugees—apparently reflects a degree of fundamental Arab denial of Israel's right to exist and of its being a legitimate Jewish state....I do not seek Israeli rule over the Temple Mount. It is a sacred place to Muslims, the mosques are facts of life, and Muslims should manage the place. I have no trouble respecting the Muslim narrative concerning the Mount/Haram. However, peace will not be established and there will be no permanent agreement on Jerusalem until an arrangement is found that will accord appropriate respect to the national Jewish narrative along with that of the Muslims.[41]

Yossi Alpher, former director of the Jaffee Center for Strategic Studies at Tel Aviv University, concluded: "Peace will not be established and there will be no permanent agreement on Jerusalem until an arrangement is found that will accord appropriate respect to the national Jewish narrative along with that of the Muslims."

Materials compiled in different books and studies by Dr. Yitzchak Reiter, Prof. Shmuel Berkovitz, and this writer[42] disclose hundreds of rulings, publications, and sources that reflect how much the denial of the Jewish connection to Jerusalem and the holy places has metastasized in the Arab world. Various Muslim elements try to undermine the Jewish principle of Jerusalem's centrality to Judaism, deny the existence of the Temple in Jerusalem, and assert that the Western Wall is not an authentic remnant of the external retaining wall of the Temple Mount compound.

The rewritten Muslim history, which challenges the Jewish link to Jerusalem and its history, makes three basic claims: that the Jewish presence in Jerusalem was short-lived (only sixty to seventy years) and does not justify Jewish sovereignty over the Holy

City; that the Temple of Solomon, which is nothing but an ancient Muslim edifice, was at most a place for personal prayer (as noted, many publications deny the Temple's existence altogether); and that the Western Wall is a sacred Muslim site, the Jewish connection to which was invented only in the nineteenth and twentieth centuries for political reasons.[43]

For example, an article posted a few years ago on the website of the northern branch of the Islamic Movement in Israel, written by Egyptian archeologist Abd al-Rahim Rihan Barakat, director of the antiquities site for the Dahab region in Sinai, states that "the legend of the fraudulent Temple is the greatest crime of historical forgery." A *fatwa* on the website of the Jerusalem Wakf asserts that David, Solomon, and Herod did not build the shrine but merely renovated a building that had already been there since the time of the first man.[44]

Today many Muslim jurists attach to the word *al-haikal* the descriptor *al-mizum*, whose literal meaning is "the alleged" or "the supposed." They thus underline their position that the Temple is an invention with no factual basis. Abd al-Tuav Mustafa, from the Department of Political Science at the University of Cairo and former presenter of a religion program on Egyptian television, wrote in a book of his that the Jews' belief in the Temple is nothing but a bogus claim and that their ostensible research is not scientific but merely conjectures and hypotheses.[45]

According to Mustafa, the Temple was a building no larger than a spacious apartment, and actually there were many other houses of worship that were dubbed "Al-Haikal." He distorts the report of the British investigatory committee on the issue of the Western Wall, which was set up in the wake of the 1929 pogroms, and tells his readers that the committee found the Jews' claim that the Western Wall is one of the walls of Solomon's Temple to be untrue (in fact, the committee's report substantiates the Jews' ancient link to the site). Mustafa purports to base himself on the research of the archeologist Prof. Kathleen Kenyon, who, he states, determined that the Jebusite city was outside the walls of Al-Haram al-Sharif in the direction of the Kidron Valley—and thus, if there was a Temple there, it did not stand where the Al-Aksa Mosque stands today. Here too one must note that the renowned archeologist, who excavated the City of David during the reign of King Hussein, did not cast doubt in her writings on the location of the Temple Mount.[46]

A similar distortion appears on the website of Israel's southern Islamic Movement. Muhammad Helaika, a member of the movement, purports to rely on Israeli archeologists in pronouncing that no vestige of the Jewish Temple has been found. Since 1967, he asserts, the Jews have conducted sixty-five archeological excavations on the Temple Mount. In actuality they have not conducted a single one because the Wakf has prevented it. Helaika quotes the archeologist Dr. Eilat Mazar as saying: "We have not reached the Temple and we have no idea where it was." Mazar, however, draws links between archeological findings and biblical and other sources that describe the Temple.[47] She, too, notes that the reason there are no findings from the Temple building itself is that no excavations could be carried out under the Temple Mount compound, the place where the Temple resided.[48]

For hundreds of years up to 1967, the story of the Jewish Temple was a firmly established and undeniable motif in Muslim literature. Classical Arab sources identify the place where the Al-Aksa Mosque stands with the place on which the Temple of Solomon stood.

Against this sweeping denial stands the fact that, for hundreds of years up to 1967, the story of the Jewish Temple—including details about it, and even information on the destruction of the First Temple by Nebuchadnezzar—was a firmly established and undeniable motif in Muslim literature of all kinds.[49] Moreover, classical Arab sources identify the place where the Al-Aksa Mosque stands with the place on which the Temple of Solomon stood. For example, the tenth-century Jerusalemite geographer and historian al-Makdisi, and the fourteenth-century Iranian jurist al-Mastufi, both identify the Al-Aksa Mosque with the Temple of Solomon. The thirteenth-century poetry of Jilal al-Din al-Rumi makes a similar identification. And Abu Bakr al-Wasiti, who was a preacher at the Al-Aksa Mosque at the beginning of the eleventh century, in his book of praises for Jerusalem adduces various traditions that mention the Temple's Jewish past.[50] One of them says that the sons of Aaron called the Rock "Al-Haikal."[51] In addition, the Supreme Muslim Council's 1924 abbreviated guide to Al-Haram al-Sharif states that "this site is one of the most ancient in the world....Its identity as the site of the Temple of Solomon is beyond all doubt."[52]

Even in the twentieth century (but before 1967) the Palestinian historian Arf al-Arf wrote that Al-Haram al-Sharif was on Mount Moriah, which, in the Book of Genesis, is the location of the threshing floor of Araunah the Jebusite, which David purchased so as to build the Temple on it. Arf al-Arf, formerly mayor of East Jerusalem, further states that Solomon built the Temple in the year 1007 BCE, and that relics from the buildings that are under the Al-Aksa Mosque date from Solomon's era. Moreover, he notes that the underground quarry next to the Nablus Gate (that is, the quarry Jews call the Cave of Tsidkiyahu [Zedekiah]) is known as "Solomon's Quarry" because David and Solomon took stones from it for the building of the Temple. But these statements were written when the Old City of Jerusalem was still part of the Kingdom of Jordan, and there is almost nothing similar in the Arab history books written since 1967 or in the discourse of today.[53]

The writings of Muslims from previous centuries contradict current claims that the Western Wall—or Al-Buraq Wall—is holy to Muslims. Indeed Muslims never created a prayer site of their own there.

As for the Western Wall—or Al-Buraq Wall for the Muslims—the writings of Muslims from previous centuries contradict current claims that this wall is holy to Muslims. Indeed Muslims never prayed there, with the exception of the Al-Buraq Mosque on the southern side of the Western Wall, and never created a prayer site of their own there. According to a survey by Dr. Shmuel Berkovitz,[54] the books and official guides on Al-Haram al-Sharif published by the Muslim Wakf in 1914, 1965, and 1990 never mention the Western Wall as a Muslim holy place. Furthermore, the *Encyclopaedia of Islam* published in 1971, in its articles on "Al-Buraq" and "Al-Haram al-Sharif," never refers to the Western Wall as a sacred site nor identifies it as the place of the tethering of Al-Buraq.[55] The "Al-Haram al-Sharif" article refers to the "Wailing Wall," a name that is identified with the tears and prayers of the Jews beside it, and no Muslim holiness is attributed to it there.[56] In his book *The History of Jerusalem in Detail*, Arf al-Arf includes the Western Wall in the list of Jewish holy places in Jerusalem and describes it in these words: "the Western Wall is the external wall of the Temple, which was renovated by Herod. And the Jews visit it often and particularly on Tisha B'Av, and when they visit it they remember the glorious and unforgettable history and begin to weep."[57]

To this contradiction between denial of the Jewish Temple and the Islamization of the Western Wall, on the one hand, and the writings of generations of Muslims themselves, on the other, must of course be added the multitude of facts, discoveries, and sources that substantiate the Jewish link to Jerusalem and the existence of the Temple. Although these are not the subject of this study, they should not go unmentioned: the Bible, the Mishnah, the Gemara, the Midrashim, and the many Jewish commentaries testify to the fact of the Temple's existence over the course of many years. To these must be added the writings of the historian Yosef ben Matityahu (Josephus Flavius),[58] who saw the Temple and its destruction with his own eyes. Josephus indeed describes the Second Temple at great length, as well as the Roman victory procession that carried

Praying at the Western Wall, 1995. After the Mughrabi Quarter was evacuated, the narrow Western Wall alley was widened into a large plaza that accommodated tens of thousands of Jewish worshippers. (Moshe Milner, Government Press Office)

the plunder of its sacred objects. This procession is also depicted on the arch that Titus had built in Rome, which commemorates the conquest of Jerusalem in 70 CE. On the Arch of Titus are pictures and reliefs of the Temple objects being borne away by Roman soldiers. In addition, the New Testament often refers to the Temple and the Temple Mount.[59] An array of archeological findings from earlier years also confirms the existence of the two Temples. Dr. Dore Gold discusses some of these testaments in *The Fight for Jerusalem*; studies by contemporary Israeli archeologists such as Dr. Gabriel Barkai, Prof. Dan Bahat, Dr. Eilat Mazar, and others deal with them in greater detail.

A catalog published by the Israel Museum[60] presents a fragment of an inscription in Greek from the Second Temple period, which was found beside the Lions' Gate of the Temple Mount. A similar, entirely preserved inscription is kept today in the Archaeology Museum in Istanbul. The inscriptions prohibit entry by non-Jews beyond the grate that surrounds the Temple and threaten transgressors with death in these terms: "No gentile will enter in from the barrier that surrounds the Temple and to the surrounding court, and whoever is caught, will be liable for his life and will die." These inscriptions are mentioned in the description of the Temple in Josephus' book *The Jewish War*.[61] In post-Six-Day War excavations along the Southern and Western walls of the Temple Mount that were conducted by Prof. Benjamin Mazar, a cornerstone was found that had stood at the southwestern corner of the Temple in Second Temple days, bearing an inscription that declares: "In the house of the shofar blast one must distinguish between sacred and profane." At this corner the priest stood when he announced the trumpet blast on Friday for the entry of Shabbat, and on Saturday evening for its departure. This is documented both in *The Jewish War* and in the Mishnah.[62]

One of the extraordinary findings of recent years, from the time of the First Temple itself, was made on the Temple Mount during the laying of electrical lines there. This was the "preserved layer of life," an underground stratum that according to archeologists "was preserved as a homogeneous whole since First Temple days. Even the shards that were identified there were broken at that very place, and have not changed their location since the days of the First Temple."[63]

Dr. Yuval Baruch, a Jerusalem-district archeologist, noted in 2008[64] that the findings in the "preserved layer of life" included pieces of tableware along with fragments of animal bones, and that the findings are dated to the eighth to ninth centuries BCE. Baruch, Prof. Ronny Reich of the University of Haifa, Prof. Yisrael Finkelstein of Tel Aviv University, and Prof. Seymour Gittin, director of the W. F. Albright Institute of Archaeological Research, tested the findings. They concluded that their nature and location could probably provide an archeological basis for the retracing of the boundaries of the Temple Mount compound in the First Temple period.[65] The findings were also sent for dating to a laboratory at the Weizmann Institute in Rehovot where identifications from the First Temple were further confirmed.[66]

Media stories on this topic agitated Muslims who for years have been denying any connection between the Jewish people and the Temple Mount, and indeed the existence of the Temple itself. The director of Jerusalem's Council for Wakf and Islamic Affairs, Azzam al-Khatib, hastened to deny the possibility of findings from the First Temple period, and said the media stories were simply aimed at bolstering the Israeli claim to sovereignty over part of the Al-Aksa compound. Member of Knesset Ibrahim Sarsur reacted similarly.[67]

A further notable finding, while not confirming the existence of the Temple, substantiates the wording of the Priestly Blessing in the Torah, a formulation the priests already used in Temple times. This is a discovery of the archeologist Dr. Gabriel Barkai: two tiny, rolled, silver scrolls, which served as amulets and contained the most ancient text of biblical Hebrew ever found, namely, verses of the Priestly Blessing from the Book of Numbers: "May the Lord bless you and keep you....May the Lord look kindly upon you and give you peace."

Yet another fascinating finding was made in rescue digs[68] carried out by the Israel Antiquities Authority a few years ago in the Ramat Shlomo neighborhood of Jerusalem. This time it was an ancient quarry that extends over at least five dunams. The dig was done in the context of a project of the City of Jerusalem to build a school for the neighborhood's children. From this quarry, giant stones were taken for use in governmental building in Second Temple-era Jerusalem. What was unique about the quarry was the tremendous size of the stones, whose length reached eight meters—similar to stones that were preserved at the lower levels of the Temple Mount compound. This is, so far, the first and only discovery of a full-size quarry that can be linked to the massive building work in Jerusalem during Second Temple times. The use of these huge stones in the building of the Temple Mount compound is what has maintained the structure's stability for two thousand years, without any need for plaster or cement. Among the dig's additional findings were coins and earthenware shards that are dated to the peak period of the building work in Second Temple days.[69]

These findings and numerous others have not altered, and apparently have only accelerated, the process of greatly augmenting Jerusalem's holiness in Islam. Jerusalem is described as having "fallen" into the hands of the Israeli Jewish sovereign. The same terminology is used for the Temple Mount mosques, which are said to have "fallen into the captivity of the Jews."[70] Their status, as we have seen, has been greatly elevated. Moreover, the Muslim narrative about Jerusalem has changed completely, now contradicting the writings and attitudes of the Muslims themselves until not many years ago. Concomitantly, the campaign to deny any Jewish link whatsoever to Jerusalem is constantly gathering steam, despite a welter of facts, sources, and archeological discoveries, many of which were acknowledged by Muslims as well until recently, and were presented in their writings in a way that is the polar opposite of how they are presented now.

Forms of the Libel: Identifying a Country with the Extremism It Fights Against

In August 2008, an animated film broadcast on Hamas' Al-Aksa TV channel showed a group of Jews, haredi in appearance (sidelocks and brimmed hats), busily digging a tunnel under the Temple Mount mosques with hoes and sledgehammers. The Jews are portrayed in the style of the Nazi newspaper *Der Stürmer*, with long, prominent noses. The focus then moves to the upper level—the plaza of the mount, above the tunnel—and there it shows a *keffiyeh*-wearing Arab, reclining and sound asleep. Again the picture goes back to the tunnel and its Jewish diggers, who are encouraging each other to persist in their labors, "but slowly, so the Arabs and the Muslims won't catch wind of it." Beside them stands an Israeli soldier who says reassuringly, "Keep digging, they're asleep." Yet the next blow of the sledgehammer shakes the earth, which cracks vertically up to the level of the mosque. A small stone, dislodged, lands on the face of the Arab who is sleeping on the plaza. He wakes up in alarm, and a title comes on the screen that warns: "Al-Aksa is in danger."[1]

The roots of Hamas, like the roots of many other agents of the "Al-Aksa is in danger" libel, draw sustenance from the messages and spirit of the Muslim Brotherhood. This movement was established in Egypt by Hasan al-Banna early in the twentieth century, and over the years it became one of the world's main movements of political Islam. The worldview of the Brotherhood posits that "Islam is the solution" for all distresses of the individual, society, and state. At the center of the Brotherhood's ideology stands the goal of an Islamic renaissance and the creation of a global caliphate, first in the Islamic countries and subsequently throughout the rest of the world, on the ruins of Western liberalism.[2] The Muslim Brotherhood denies Israel's right to exist and views all the land of Palestine as an Islamic endowment (Wakf). They too are partners in the "Al-Aksa is in danger" libel, and in August 2006 Muhammad Mahdi Akef, a former leader of the movement,[3] spoke of "Al-Aksa Mosque that is captive in the hands of the accursed Zionists...who want to destroy it and build the Temple on its ruins."[4]

The Muslim Brotherhood and Hamas, which remains its official Palestine arm,[5] are not the only ones making such claims. In the spring of 2005, then-prime minister Ariel Sharon addressed the issue of the honoring of agreements by Arab leaders. In response, the Jordanian press attacked Israel harshly. On March 19 *Al-Rai* published a cartoon in which snakes are climbing on the mosque on the Temple Mount. Next month the same newspaper published another cartoon with an octopus clutching the dome of the Al-Aksa Mosque in its tentacles. At the center of the octopus is a Star of David. The use of a snake and an octopus was not accidental. The identification of Jews with octopuses and snakes has been common in different versions of *The Protocols of the Elders of Zion* since the start of the twentieth century. Octopuses and snakes indeed appear frequently in anti-Semitic cartoons and publications in the Arab world.[6]

In July 2010, Jordan's *Al-Doustur* published another atrocious caricature: a Jew with a satanic gaze is gobbling an ice cream cone in the image of the Al-Aksa Mosque.[7] And two days later another cartoon showed a Jew devouring a cake in the form of the Al-Aksa Mosque, while beside him stands an Arab who is looking at his watch.[8]

Another libeler was the head preacher at the Al-Aksa Mosque, and indeed the senior Islamic legal scholar in the Palestinian Authority in the early 2000s, Jerusalem mufti Sheikh Akrama Sabri. Born in 1939, he was already an extremist member of the Muslim Brotherhood while Jordan ruled the West Bank. In 2000, in an interview with the Egyptian weekly *Al-Ahram*,[9] Sheikh Sabri said he thought that the Muslims "still have not sacrificed enough for the liberation of Al-Aksa. Saladin sacrificed a great deal and over a long period so as to liberate Jerusalem, and we must sacrifice until Allah's victory is realized." The sheikh took the same opportunity to clarify his attitude toward the Jews: "I enter the Al-Aksa Mosque with head held high and at the same time filled with wrath against the Jews. I have never wished a Jew peace, nor anything else when I have passed one of them. I will never do so. They can't even imagine such a greeting from me."[10]

Two years later, in August 2002, a booklet by Sabri called "Palestine: The People and the Land" was published in Egypt.[11] This pamphlet, too, revealed the mufti's views. Its main message is the lack of any right of the Jewish people to the Land of Israel and a total delegitimization of the State of Israel. Sabri uses anti-Semitic motifs in his writings that are taken from the *Protocols*; he speaks of "the schemes of the Jews not only to take over Palestine but the whole world as well, by fomenting conflicts between the different countries." Sabri, who has stressed in the past that "the Western Wall, Al-Buraq, was not a place of worship for the Jews and the Jews' claim to a right to it is fraudulent,"[12] warned already in January 1997 of "the collapse of the Al-Aksa Mosque within two years at the most." He ascribed this to the Israeli excavations "that are being conducted beneath its foundations, from 1967 to the present."[13]

Sabri's successor as mufti of Jerusalem, Sheikh Muhammad Hussein, was no less enterprising. He charged that "at the top of the order of priorities of plans of conquest and aggression" stood the Al-Aksa Mosque; its existence annoyed Israel, which aimed to build the "bogus" Temple on its ruins.[14] Like his predecessor, Hussein denied the Jewish link to the Western Wall and referred to Israel's "frightening and terror-inducing plans" regarding the Western Wall plaza.[15]

These examples are not anomalous. The ones who have developed and refined the "Al-Aksa is in danger" incitement campaign almost into a fine art are Sheikh Raed Salah and his northern branch of the Israeli Islamic Movement, which is an arm of the Muslim Brotherhood and close to Hamas (see Chapter 6), but they are not the only ones. Hasan Tahub, one of the heads of the Supreme Muslim Council and subsequently appointed Wakf minister by Arafat, promised in an interview with *Al-Hayat al-Jadida*[16] that he would

> prevent anyone who is not a Muslim from praying at Al-Aksa Mosque, even if it requires the use of force. Al-Aksa is a Muslim mosque according to a divine decree that is more important than the decisions of any court. The permission that was granted a Jewish extremist to pray at the Al-Aksa Mosque was an Israeli attempt to gain a foothold in it, so that in the future they can erect the Temple that they claim once existed on this spot.

It should be noted that the Israeli courts did not provide permits, neither to moderate nor extremist Jews, to pray at the Al-Aksa Mosque.[17] (See Chapter 2.)

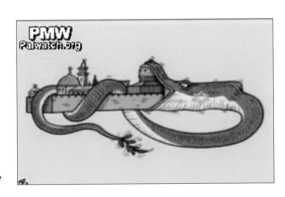

The president of the Sharia Court in Nablus, Sheikh Hamed Bitawi, also characterized Al-Aksa as being "in danger, because Israel, both the government and the people, is resolute in its aim to destroy it and build its bogus shrine in its place."[18] The deputy Wakf minister of the Palestinian Authority, Sheikh Yusuf Juma Salama, alleged—again without basis—that when the Israelis "first entered Jerusalem in 1967, they would say, when they were inside the Al-Aksa Mosque: Muhammad is dead, dead. Muhammad left daughters behind him."[19] And in the same period of the late 1990s, Muhammad Awad, sheikh of the branch of Al-Azhar University in Gaza, asserted: "the law determines that the *jihad* for the liberation of the Al-Aksa Mosque and Jerusalem constitutes a personal duty that is incumbent on every Muslim man and woman."[20]

Statements in a similar spirit also were made by Zahir al-Dibai, master of ceremonies for the marking of "The Night Journey and the Prophet's Ascent to Heaven" at the Al-Haj Nimr Mosque in Nablus in the presence of Arafat. "Our Palestinian nation and people under your leadership," al-Dibai declared, "have never hesitated to defend Jerusalem and to sacrifice young people and clear, pure blood in Talbieh, in Katamon, in Baka,[21] at the Al-Aksa Mosque, on the Via Dolorosa and everywhere, since all of us obey the call of Allah."[22] Al-Dibai hitched Christian sites, too, such as the Via Dolorosa, to his proclamation on behalf of "the campaign for the Al-Aksa Mosque."

Almost a decade later nothing has changed. Indeed, a survey by Palestinian Media Watch after a temporary spike in terror attacks in Jerusalem revealed that the Palestinian media, including in eastern Jerusalem, wages a ceaseless campaign of fear-mongering about Jerusalem that affects Muslims and Palestinians generally and the Arab residents of Jerusalem in particular.[23] Beyond accusing Israel of "ethnic cleansing" and even

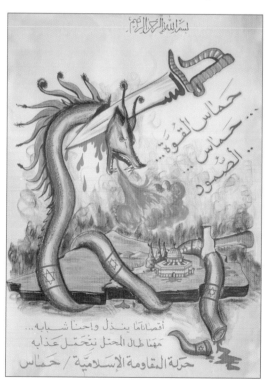

A dragon adorned with Stars of David breathes fire on the Dome of the Rock. A greeting card from Hamas to the Palestinian people, found in a mosque during Operation Defensive Shield, 2002. (Tsvika Israeli, Government Press Office)

of spreading rats and drugs among the Arab population, Israel is portrayed as jeopardizing the holy places and concocting schemes to destroy the Al-Aksa Mosque. In making these charges the Palestinian media and the Authority used a terminology of fear, various libels, and exhortations by different leaders. Other common admonitions were that "Israel is building an underground Jewish city"[24] and "erecting a bridge that will hold hundreds of soldiers and police along with vehicles, so that they can break into the Al-Aksa Mosque."[25] And, not least, that Jewish extremists were planning to bring "missile launchers to the Old City of conquered Jerusalem" for the purpose of "bombarding the Al-Aksa Mosque with missiles."[26]

It should be pointed out that Israel is not building an underground Jewish city, and at most is carrying out organized archeological excavations under the supervision of the Israel Antiquities Authority. These excavations are open to everyone, and even Wakf officials and Muslim clergy have been invited more than once to visit them, and sometimes even accepted the invitations. The bridge in question, which is supposed to allow "breaking into the Al-Aksa Mosque," is the wooden bridge that leads to the Mughrabi Gate. This bridge was built in 2004 after the storms of winter, along with a mild earthquake, had collapsed the earthen ramp that had led to the gate. The plan was to build in its stead a more stable bridge made of metal, which could support greater weight and serve the security forces in times of emergency—certainly not for the purpose of breaking into Al-Aksa for its own sake, but, rather, for restoring public order to the Temple Mount in case of disturbances. When the police had broken into the mount in the past, it was to put down violent outbursts by Muslims there in which they hurled rocks at Jews praying at the Western Wall below. The bridge, then, is intended to replace the ramp that collapsed, enable access to the mount, and serve the Israeli security forces when they need to restrain Palestinian lawbreakers on the mount.

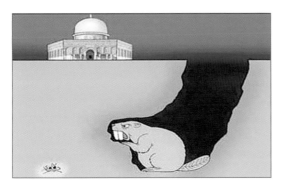

Palestinian publications, however, maliciously distorted all of this. Only the warning about a plan by Jewish extremists to fire missiles had a basis. In the past, intelligence information about an intention of that kind has indeed reached the Israel Police—which, of course, along with other security forces, made certain to thwart it.[27] But this simple truth did not deter the supreme kadi (judge) of the Palestinians, Sheikh al-Tamimi, from accusing the City of Jerusalem of wanting to renovate the Mughrabi ramp so as to "enable more than five thousand occupation soldiers and an Israeli tank force to enter the plaza of the Al-Aksa Mosque, in futile attempts to search for their supposed shrine."[28]

The exploitation of chance occurrences, whether trivial or more serious, to spread the "Al-Aksa is in danger" lie and affix it firmly to the State of Israel was not exceptional and indeed became routine. Usually this was done in the context of excavations in the vicinity of the Temple Mount, even if these were conducted hundreds of meters from it, and even if they involved construction work that was carried out at the height level of the Temple Mount mosque itself (see Chapter 6).

The libel never distinguishes between private, extremist, non-institutional actors who are marginal to Israeli society, and the State of Israel that does so much to prevent harm to the mosques and safeguard them.

Although there is sometimes a factual basis to trigger concern, the libel never distinguishes between private, extremist, non-institutional actors who are marginal to Israeli society, and the State of Israel that does so much to prevent harm to the mosques and safeguard them. Only once, in the course of the 1967 war, did an official Israeli actor speak of harming the mosques, but the response of the senior military commander in the field was unequivocally clear and negative. The former was Rabbi Shlomo Goren, who was chief military rabbi at the time. The latter was the then head of IDF Central Command, Uzi Narkiss, who threatened him with arrest and imprisonment. Subsequently Goren denied that he had considered such a possibility, and even explained that, in his view, such an idea would be pointless.[29]

Since then, several extremists and fanatics (mostly Jews) have attempted to attack the mosques and been thwarted by the state. In the first decade and a half after the Six-Day War, would-be perpetrators who were apprehended included the Jewish Underground, Yoel Lerner, and members of the Lifta gang.[30] Later, on two occasions in the 2000s, there were further surprises.[31] Those responsible were caught, tried, and put behind bars. Sometimes the people in question suffered from a mental condition known as the Jerusalem syndrome. Mostly Christians, they were captured in time and put in mental institutions for treatment.[32] Nevertheless, the Muslim side pinned the blame for these incidents on the Israeli government and said it was behind them.

This failure to make a fundamental distinction was especially evident in two unfortunate cases. The first occurred in August 1969 when an Australian Christian tourist named Michael Dennis Rohan entered the Al-Aksa Mosque and tried to set it on fire.[33] Rohan fled, but he was caught and found unfit to stand trial; the court stated that at the time of his act he was "gravely afflicted with a mental illness that is defined as paranoid schizophrenia."[34] Rohan suffered from delusions that had taken control of his life. He was confined to a mental institution and, in 1974 after pressures from his family, deported from Israel. Yet his capture, and confession of his deed, had no impact on the anti-Israeli incitement campaign that was waged in the Arab and Muslim world over the arson attack at Al-Aksa. The president of Egypt, Gamal Abdel Nasser, called for a "purification" war against Israel. In Saudi Arabia, King Faisal called on all Muslims to mobilize for a *jihad* against Israel; appeals for *jihad* against the Jewish state were heard in almost every Arab country. In all cases Israel was accused of having planned the deed. Many years later, in Egypt, an official propaganda booklet ("Jerusalem Is an Arab City") was published in English and French whose core theme was that "Israel planned the arson attack on Al-Aksa in September 1969":

Israel gained control over East Jerusalem and immediately began [archeological] investigations near Al-Aksa, claiming it was searching for ancient Jewish relics. However, Israel's aim was to damage the Muslim holy places so that it could eventually remove them, pursuant to the Judaization of the whole area....To fulfill its goals, Israel planned to set fire to the Al-Aksa Mosque on September 18, 1969.[35]

The book made no mention, not even a word, of the Australian lunatic Rohan, who set fire to the mosque, was apprehended, and was charged for his deeds. Similarly to how the "Western Wall conflict" was exploited by Haj Amin al-Husseini in the early twentieth century, the Rohan incident was leveraged to organize huge fundraising campaigns for the mosques and their courts, which lasted for decades after the event.

The Muslims took a similar approach when, in 1982, Alan Goodman, an Israeli soldier, broke into the Temple Mount and shot dead a Muslim guard. Goodman, too, was quickly apprehended and in his interrogation stated a clear motive for his act: revenge for the murder of almost forty Jews by Palestinian terrorists on the Coastal Road four years earlier. Goodman gave the impression of treading a fine line between sanity and madness. His trial mostly focused on the question of his sanity, and he was found to be suffering from borderline personality disorder. Although some psychiatrists asserted that he also had paranoid schizophrenia, Goodman was ultimately found fit to stand trial and sentenced to life in prison.

The standard ritual occurred in this case, too. The Muslims—the Wakf, the Supreme Muslim Council, the Arab states—blamed Israel. Yasser Arafat announced that "it was the Israeli government that dispatched Alan Goodman to the Temple Mount so as to carry out an ugly crime and a religious stratagem."[36] The mufti of Jerusalem, Sheikh Saad al-Din al-Alami, had his own version of what happened, saying it did not accord (to put it mildly) with what had emerged during Goodman's trial. "Goodman did not act alone," claimed the sheikh,

> his act was part of a planned operation of a large group of Jews, in which soldiers also took part. At exactly the same moment that Goodman began to fire, shots were fired at the Dome of the Rock toward a group of Muslims who were standing there, coming from three other directions...just at that moment we were also fired at from the Jewish Quarter. And from the Mount of Olives as well, and also from a nearby building that is in the army's hands. It was planned. Organized.

Sheikh al-Almi's account was entirely imaginary with no basis in reality. The Shin Bet and the Israel Police looked into the matter thoroughly and found that Goodman had acted alone. In an official announcement, the Israeli government expressed its sorrow and apologized for the incident.

It is worth noting here that when, on March 13, 1997, a Jordanian soldier in Naharayim in the Jordan Valley fired on a group of girls from the Israeli town of Beit Shemesh who were touring the area, murdering seven of them, Israel did not even consider accusing the Kingdom of Jordan of organizing and planning the incident. Israel accepted the apology of Jordan's King Hussein, who expressed sorrow for the massacre in the name of his kingdom. Nor did Israel even consider accusing the Egyptian government of organizing and planning the incident of October 5, 1985, in which an Egyptian soldier opened fire with an automatic weapon at a group of Israeli tourists staying at the Ras Burka resort in Sinai. The soldier, who was part of a regular security consignment in the area, murdered seven Israelis before his companions were able to overcome him.

Just as the Rohan and Goodman incidents were exploited to fan the flames, incite against Israel, and accuse it of plotting to destroy the mosques, the same tack was taken over the years on much less severe matters than attempted attacks on the Temple Mount by Jewish extremists. Sometimes no excuse at all was needed to level such accusations against Israel. Generally, intellectual activity as in conferences, or demonstrations by supporters of Jewish access to the mount—most of whom are not weavers of plots to demolish the mosques but who seek to preserve the Jewish link to the site—sufficed to enable the inciters to concoct a web of conspiracy theories.

Many Muslims have attributed the attempted attacks by Jewish extremists, or the activity of the Temple Mount movements, to the Israeli establishment (rabbinical, political, and security). They have portrayed these institutions as lurking behind the extremist elements. In their view it is all one mechanism in which different actors participate, each playing a different role. For them the facts are of no relevance at all. Over the years the Israeli authorities have foiled several attacks and planned attacks on the mosques by Jewish extremists or disordered people (both Christians and Jews). Even national-religious Jews with a clear, evident affinity to the mount, but who also understand the significance of damaging its mosques, have more than once passed information to the security forces when they feared such a possibility.[37] Nevertheless, the aim of attacking Al-Aksa is almost always attributed to the Israeli state and its institutions.[38]

November 18, 2007.
Alaa al-Laqta, Falestin
(Hamas), Intelligence
and Terrorism
Information Center

The "Al-Aksa is in danger" libelers also ignore the high price that Israel has paid, both practically and in terms of sentiments and values, to protect the holy places of Islam in Jerusalem. This price has included, as we have seen, religious autonomy for Muslims at the most holy site of the Jewish people, difficult visiting restrictions for Jews, and the prohibition of Jewish prayer at the site. The State of Israel has, moreover, diminished the stature of the Temple Mount and placed the emphasis on the Western Wall, despite the fact that the latter is actually only a retaining wall of the former, while it is the mount that was the focal point of Jewish life for many generations, and the place where the two Temples existed and were destroyed.

In 2000, a few months after the Second Intifada broke out, Sheikh Yusuf al-Qaradawi, one of the most popular muftis in the Muslim world today and the leading religious authority in the eyes of the Muslim Brotherhood, said that "the danger to Al-Aksa is now greater than ever...and hence the Muslims of the world must arise and defend it because it is not the property of the Palestinians alone but of the whole Muslim nation, just as Mecca does not belong to Saudi Arabia alone but to the whole Muslim world."[39] A short time later the newspaper *Al-Asra'a*[40] (published by the office of the Palestinian mufti) offered a graphic illustration of Qaradawi's words: a poster showing a Palestinian child mocking an armed Israeli soldier against the background of the Al-Aksa Mosque. The poster carries the legend: "Safeguarding the Al-Aksa Mosque—the duty of 1,300,000,000 Muslims." It was disseminated that same year at the Arab Book Fair in Cairo, and a large Muslim public in Egypt and other Muslim countries was exposed to it.[41]

Left: Poster from the website of the Izzadin al-Kassam Brigades with the caption "No to the Judaization of the Al-Aksa Mosque." (Intelligence and Terrorism Information Center)

Right: Poster published on Hamas' website with the heading "For your sake, o Al-Aksa," from an article of February 6, 2007. Israel is accused of aiming to destroy the Al-Aksa Mosque and build the Temple in its stead.

To the "Al-Aksa is in danger" campaign was added a further motif of recapitulating a seminal event from Jerusalem's Muslim past—the victory of the commander Saladin over the Crusaders in 1187 at Karnei Hittin, and his subsequent triumphant entry to Jerusalem. The undisguised hope is that in our time, too, another Saladin will arise who will liberate Jerusalem and its holy places from Jewish rule. This theme appears in many works from the time of the intifada, and is widespread up to the present day.

A picture by Rajaa Yusuf Salamat, 12, from Nablus. The "snake," an anti-Semitic symbol for Jews (in the picture it has a kippa and sidelocks), is trying to swallow the Dome of the Rock as blood drips from its mouth and from the building. Found during Operation Defensive Shield, 2002. (Intelligence and Terrorism Information Center)

Many Muslims perceive Saladin's expulsion of the Crusaders as analogous to what happened during the intifada: Jerusalem is indeed in the hands of the Jews, not the Christians, but their fate is to be the same. Both are seen as a foreign implantation in the region,[42] and the trauma of the 1967 Six-Day War is analogous to Jerusalem's conquest by the Crusaders in 1099. At the end of the twentieth century, when the nine hundredth anniversary of Saladin's triumph was celebrated throughout the Muslim world, the Association of Arab Historians convened in Baghdad to mark the event in honor of Jerusalem. There the sentiments were expressed officially. The conference ended with an announcement on "the need to liberate Jerusalem from the Zionist defilement, as Saladin did when he purified it of the Crusader defilement."[43]

The new Muslim ethos has also been assimilated in childhood and adolescent education. In a workbook for children, Jimla Natur, a Jerusalem resident who was born before 1948 and spent her girlhood there in the San Simon neighborhood, wrote: "The Crusaders... did not succeed to become part of the region, their kingdom declined and the remnants of the conquerors returned to Europe. We have no doubt. History repeats itself with astonishing precision. Most of the Jews, too, came from Europe...the end of the road for the Zionist state will resemble the fate of the Crusader Kingdom. All we lack is a Saladin of today."[44]

Also addressing children as a target public for the new ethos was the quiz "Jerusalem in Danger," published online by the Committee for Islamic Heritage and the Al-Aksa Association for Assistance to the Wakf and Islamic Sites. The two bodies operate from the Israeli Arab town of Umm al-Fahm and are linked to the northern branch of the Islamic Movement. As the introduction to the quiz explains:

> In this competition you will learn about the dangers that lie in wait for Jerusalem, the Al-Aksa Mosque, and the Dome of the Rock. In the competition you will learn about the Jewish schemes to Judaize the city in stages. In the competition you will learn about the enemies of our holy places and the enemies of our faith. In this competition you will learn about the enemy's attitude toward us. This will help you in building your attitude toward him.

After these introductory words come maxims by different religious sages, and then come the questions themselves. Question 55 expresses to the full, it appears, the outlook of the authors of the quiz. The question describes the archeological excavations that Israel is carrying out near the Temple Mount, and the contestants have to choose among several possibilities, only one of which—or perhaps all of them, the authors say—is right:

The Jewish scheme to build what is called the Temple began:

1. Two months after the intifada
2. After the conquest of East Jerusalem in 1967
3. At the end of the nineteenth century
4. Since the Persian king Cyrus returned the Jews to Jerusalem[45]

The book by Yitzchak Reiter, *From Jerusalem to Mecca and Back*, notes another activity for the young: a Monopoly game board for children that was purchased in a Muslim neighborhood in Sydney. The title of the game is "The Way to Jerusalem"; at the center of the board is a picture of the Dome of the Rock with a Palestinian flag atop it. The players, who are equipped with different weapons, have to conquer Jerusalem, but first have to take over Eilat, Hebron, and Tel Aviv. Another visual item—the Dome of the Rock with a crying eye at its center—appears on the cover of the book *Jerusalem: Faith and History*.[46] And these are just a few examples out of thousands of written publications, websites, textbooks for teenagers and adults, newspaper items, sermons, and various media, all of which can be included under the rubric "Al-Aksa is in danger."

This campaign of fear resonates much more than did the activities of Mufti Haj Amin al-Husseini during the Mandate period; it has been internalized to the point that almost no one questions it any longer. In his book *Arab Political Myths*, published over twenty years ago, Prof. Emanuel Sivan relates the story of Sadik Jalal al-Azm, a young Syrian intellectual whose book *Self-Criticism after the Defeat* explored the reasons for the calamity that the Arab states suffered at Israel's hands in the Six-Day War. Al-Azm stirred up a storm in the Muslim world by maintaining that the ultimate source of the defeat was the profound influence of religion on the Arab soul; among other evidence for this point he cited "the Arab obsession with Jerusalem falling into Israel's hands." Today, however, even singular phenomena such as that of Sadik Jalal al-Azm have almost ceased to exist. Also extremely anomalous is the position of Abd al-Hadi Palazzi, one of the leaders of the Muslim community in Italy. Palazzi states publicly that the Temple Mount does not have a special status of holiness.[47]

Even a balanced view, as in an article by Prof. Sari Nusseibeh, president of Al-Quds University, is extremely unusual. The article in question presents a historical challenge to the wars that are waged over holy places, and also grants recognition to the Jewish narrative of Jerusalem and the Temple Mount. Nusseibeh, one of the well-regarded intellectuals in Palestinian society, writes among other things: "The Lord conferred holiness on the land of Canaan, and designated it for the children of Israel; the legendary Temple of Jerusalem was at the spot where the Shekhinah dwelt and there the great priests served the Lord."[48] Nusseibeh is critical, however, of how people relate to the holy places: "It is hard for me to see how God could feel better when human beings kill and are killed over this holy place and each man destroys his neighbor." In Nusseibeh's view, it is human beings themselves who, over time, have raised the level of holiness of places such as the Dome of the Rock or the Kaaba in Mecca.

But opinions such as those of al-Azm, Palazzi, or Nusseibeh are extremely rare. For most of the Muslim world, "Al-Aksa is in danger" is not just a slogan but a reality; a fact that cannot be questioned.

Sheikh Raed Salah as Successor of the Mufti Haj Amin al-Husseini

If in the first three decades after the Six-Day War it was Jordan and the Palestinians who set the tone on the Temple Mount,[1] each making use of the "Al-Aksa is in danger" slogan to build up their status as leaders in the struggle to protect and liberate Jerusalem, beginning in the mid-1990s Sheikh Raed Salah appropriated this issue as his own.

Sheikh Raed Salah, head of the northern branch of the Israeli Islamic Movement. He became the successor of Haj Amin al-Husseini, refurbished the "Al-Aksa is in danger" libel, incited violence, and promised to redeem Al-Aksa "in fire and blood." (Tara Todras-Whitehill, Associated Press)

It was Salah and his Israeli Islamic Movement, and particularly its northern branch, who during 1996-1998 brought about the very substantial change in the status quo that had prevailed on the Temple Mount since 1967, and indeed since the days of the mufti Haj Amin al-Husseini, who renovated the mosques in the 1920s and 1930s. Salah and his movement prepared prayer rugs for the extensive underground space, known as Solomon's Stables, in the southeastern corner of the mount, and for the space under the Al-Aksa Mosque (or "ancient Al-Aksa"). They turned these into two additional mosques. One of them, the new mosque in Solomon's Stables, extends for 4,500 meters and is actually one of the largest mosques ever built in Israel.

Salah also launched an effort to clean out the cisterns on the Temple Mount and almost succeeded to implement a plan to import water from the holy Well of Zamzam in Mecca, which would have enhanced the place's status even more[2] as well as his own. Success in this would have bestowed him with the status of the *saki* (who sprinkles the pilgrims with holy water) and the *sadan* (beadle), roles that are traditionally reserved for descendants of the Prophet Muhammad at the pilgrimage site in Mecca.

Without a doubt, Salah is the disciple par excellence of Husseini, a pupil who outdoes his teacher: Salah has ramped up the "Al-Aksa is in danger" libel to a pitch that his forerunners and competitors have not reached. He has done so both by using crude, violent language to convey radical messages against the State of Israel, the Jews, and the Zionist movement, and through huge annual gatherings and worldwide fundraising campaigns for his movement's Al-Aksa Association for Defense of the Holy Places.[3] Salah, who has been closely tied to the Muslim Brotherhood and influenced by its ideology, has also been in contact with Sheikh Yusuf al-Qaradawi and Hamas leader Dr. Mahmoud al-Zahar, and he led delegations of his movement to meet with Hamas founder Sheikh Ahmed Yassin.[4]

In September 1996 and in September 1997 in Umm al-Fahm, Salah's power base,[5] the Islamic Movement held its first two mass rallies under the "Al-Aksa is in danger" slogan. The second rally was held in the wake of what came to be known as the Western Wall Tunnel riots, a bloody event that the Palestinians instigated over the opening of a northern exit gate for the Western Wall Tunnel (see Chapter 9). The gate provided visitors and tourists in the tunnel with access to the Via Dolorosa and the Muslim markets of the Old City, instead of having to retrace their steps within the narrow tunnel and return to the Western Wall plaza. Yet, according to accusations leveled by the Palestinian Authority and the Islamic Movement, behind this measure lurked an Israeli plan to bring down the Temple Mount mosques. In the ensuing riots fifteen IDF soldiers and forty Palestinians were killed, and hundreds of others injured. It was under the impetus of these riots that the work on Solomon's Stables and, indeed, the process of turning them into a mosque was greatly speeded up and completed.

In the first two "Al-Aksa is in danger" rallies, a model of the Dome of the Rock could be seen behind the speaker's podium. Its dome was painted red, a symbol of its travails at the hands of the Jews. Already evident in these rallies was the tack taken ever since by the Islamic Movement and its leader Raed Salah. The chairman of the Higher Monitoring Committee of the Israeli Arab sector, Ibrahim Nimr Hussein, declared that "in Jerusalem there is no vestige of Judaism. It is Muslim and it is our duty to defend it with all our might." The mufti of Jerusalem at that time, Sheikh Akrama Sabri, also proclaimed that "the Muslims will defend Jerusalem with their lives."[6]

Four years later came the outbreak of the Al-Aksa Intifada, which took a toll, for Jews and Arabs, of thousands dead and over ten thousand injured. The Palestinians claim the intifada broke out because of the visit by Ariel Sharon, then leader of the Likud opposition, to the Temple Mount on September 28, 2000. In line with the Palestinians' demand, the visit was conducted outside of the mosque and was in fact coordinated with the Palestinian Authority. That did not, however, prevent the incitement and bloodshed that came in its wake.[7] Sharon was described as a murderer who was defiling the Muslim holy places.[8] Again the Muslims were called on to defend Al-Aksa and Jerusalem, and this time too the justification was that Israel aimed to destroy the mosques and build the Third Temple in their place. Later Amad al-Paluji, who was a minister in the Palestinian government, said that two months before Sharon's visit to the mount, in the immediate aftermath of the failed Israeli-Palestinian talks at Camp David, the intifada was already being planned. Israeli intelligence also found evidence of this,[9] though at the time it was kept under wraps.

The intifada, which lasted several years, began at the end of September 2000. Its first days saw demonstrations and violent riots by Arab citizens of Israel. These began with mass rallies expressing Israeli Arabs' solidarity with Palestinians in the territories. Roads were blocked and demonstrators began clashing with police contingents. Ultimately twelve Israeli Arabs, one Palestinian who was not an Israeli citizen, and one Israeli Jew were killed in the October riots in northern Israel.

Complying with a demand by the Israeli Arab leadership, the government of Prime Minister Ehud Barak set up a state commission of inquiry chaired by Judge Theodore Or. The commission harshly criticized government ministers, police officials, and leaders of the Israeli Arab sector and particularly Raed Salah and members of his movement.

The members of the commission[10]—Judges Theodore Or and Hashem Khatib, and Prof. Shimon Shamir—singled out the Islamic Movement's involvement with the issue of the Temple Mount. They noted that "in the Islamic Movement's activity [with regard to the mount], more than in other areas, its strategy emerged clearly: escalating conflict, activism in the field, and agitating the public. The movement gave Al-Aksa priority as a sensitive focal point for unifying the Muslims in Israel, and as a bridge to the Palestinian society in the territories and to the Islamic world as a whole."[11]

The Or Commission that investigated the Israeli Arab riots in October 2000 found that "it is not credible that Sheikh Salah actually believed that the Israeli government intended to destroy the mosques and build the Temple in their place, as he claimed."

The commission stated that

> even though there is no doubt about the profound religious sentiments of Sheikh Raed Salah and his genuine concern about Muslim control of Al-Aksa...it is not credible that Sheikh Salah actually believed that the Israeli government intended to destroy the mosques and build the Temple in their place, as he claimed. *There is no escaping the conclusion that his assertions on this matter were aimed at amassing political capital—at mobilizing supporters and escalating conflict.* His calls to liberate Al-Aksa at the price of blood, especially as voiced in the massive and impassioned rallies that he organized, were responsible for further aggravating

the tense atmosphere in the Arab sector before the events of October (emphasis added).[12]

Indeed, an examination of the testimonies, speeches, and declarations—the actions and the atmosphere that Salah generated—makes clear how the judges, one of them an Israeli Arab from Nazareth, arrived at these conclusions.

Already in the violent al-Ruha events of 1998,[13] Salah had incited behavior of the sort that erupted in October 2000. Salah already saw those events as an "encouraging attempt," and he egged on the demonstrators with incendiary rhetoric. In an interview in 1999, Salah called on the Arab public to cease being reactive and instead turn proactive and confrontational.[14] Soon after, he called on the residents to physically block the setting up of army camps on parts of the al-Ruha lands (located in the mostly Arab-populated Wadi Ara area). He continued to threaten violence at the Land Day gathering in March 2000.

The Or Commission notes that Salah's call to the public to protect Al-Aksa invoked, among other things, the attitudes of Jewish extremist groups: "rabbis and politicians who broached various plans for building a synagogue on the mount. A number of extremist groups have engaged in demonstrative and symbolic acts of fulfilling the vision of the rebuilt Temple, and in the context of political negotiations different plans have been raised that aimed to strengthen the status of the Jews on the mount." The commission went on to assert, however, that *"Raed Salah went much further, since he acted to stir up the Arab public against a supposed intention of the Israeli government to replace the Al-Aksa mosques[15] with a Jewish Temple—an intention that had no connection whatsoever to reality* (emphasis added)."[16]

How did Salah do this?

Here, too, it is worth relying on the commission's report, which examined written materials and interrogated numerous witnesses including Raed Salah himself. Salah called to sacrifice human lives for the sake of protecting Al-Aksa. He also endorsed the updated Muslim tenet that the Al-Aksa Mosque also includes the Western Wall. As far as Salah is concerned, even the existence of the police station on the Temple Mount compound,[17] that is, the presence of Israeli policing at the site, puts Al-Aksa in danger.[18]

At the 1999 "Al-Aksa is in danger" rally, a senior figure in Salah's movement said that "the oil lamp of Al-Aksa could be extinguished, but we are prepared to light Al-Aksa with blood, because he who lights it with his blood will not be extinguished."[19] The messages at the annual gathering in 2000 were no different. At that event Sheikh Salah characterized any assertion of any Jewish right whatsoever to the Temple Mount as a declaration of religious war on all Muslims; as he put it:

We will say openly to the Jewish society, you do not have a right even to one stone of the blessed Al-Aksa Mosque. You do not have a right even to one tiny particle of the blessed Al-Aksa Mosque. Therefore we will say openly, *the western wall of blessed Al-Aksa is part of blessed Al-Aksa*. It can never be a small Western Wall. It can never be a large Western Wall.... We will say openly to the political and religious leadership in Israel: *the demand to keep blessed Al-Aksa under Israeli sovereignty is also a declaration of war on the Islamic world* (emphasis added).[20]

During the rally Sheikh Salah led chants of "In spirit, in blood, we will redeem you Al-Aksa."[21] Similar statements were made by a senior activist in the Islamic Movement's northern branch, who attributed to then-prime minister Barak an intention to destroy the Al-Aksa Mosque so as to build the Temple on its ruins. He threatened that tears would not be shed for Al-Aksa because blood would flow for it. He also likened Barak, with his alleged aim of toppling Al-Aksa and erecting the Temple in its stead, to Abraha al-Ashram, the Ethiopian military leader who, according to Muslim tradition based on the Elephant Sura (Sura 105) of the Koran, came to Mecca with the goal of destroying the Kaaba stone. Allah, however, sent a flock of birds after him who threw stones at him and his followers, breaking his neck. This activist said Barak should know that Allah could, in the present as well, dispatch a flock of birds of that kind; or, if not, the Muslims themselves would fulfill Allah's decree. This same individual, publisher of the northern branch's periodical, also made these assertions at greater length in an article there.[22] Salah himself, in an interview a few days earlier, made similar claims about the Barak-led government's ostensible plans to build the Temple.[23]

Salah, an Israeli citizen, related to Israel as to an enemy state. About a month and a half before the October riots, the Islamic Movement's *Tsut al-Chak v'al-Huriya* printed a poem by him on the destruction of a house of prayer, apparently at Sarafend on Habonim Beach (in northern Israel), by the Jews.[24] The poem casts the Jews as the enemy of Allah, destined for annihilation. While this enemy of Allah to which the poem refers—as the Or Commission also realized—is not explicitly identified with Israel, it is hard not to understand it that way, or at least to claim that the Arab readers of the poem would understand it differently.[25]

Two days after the Al-Aksa Intifada broke out, at the start of October 2000, the National Shura (Consultative) Council of the Islamic Movement published an announcement on the killing of the Palestinians a day earlier at the Al-Aksa plaza. This announcement, which Salah himself formulated, lauded the sacrifice of blood on Al-Aksa's behalf.[26] In another announcement a month later, the Islamic Movement made clear that it regarded a further incident on the Temple Mount on October 29, 2000, in which four Palestinians were killed, as a "planned massacre" pure and simple. Salah had already offered his own angle on the bloodshed in an article on October 6, 2000. There he dubbed the bloody strife since the end of September as the "Al-Aksa Intifada," and praised it as an uprising in which the Arabs of the land had made the Al-Aksa Mosque their common cause.

In February 2007, Salah gave a sermon that was even more extreme. The context of his statements was the ongoing rescue digs of the Israel Antiquities Authority outside the Temple Mount near the Mughrabi Gate access ramp, where an earthen ramp had collapsed due to natural causes (see Chapter 9). Speaking in the Wadi Joz neighborhood of Jerusalem, Salah reiterated that Israel was aiming to build the Temple in place of the Al-Aksa Mosque and added: "What audacity have they to build a house of prayer... when our blood is still on their clothes, on their doors, in their food and drink? Our blood passes from one terrorist general to another terrorist general." Salah also repeated demented anti-Semitic claims he had made previously in the spirit of the blood libel of medieval Europe: "We are not a nation that is based on hate. It is not we who have ever allowed ourselves to eat bread soaked in the blood of children....Soon Islam will rule the entire Middle East in the form of a caliphate state [i.e., a religious Muslim state] that will uphold the honor of Jewish synagogues."[27]

Over two years later, in November 2009, Salah again raised the idea of the caliphate and surmised that "not far is the day when Al-Quds will be a global Muslim capital of a global Islamic caliphate."[28] In May 2010, Member of Knesset Masud Ganaim of the United Arab List-Taal faction, who is a member of the Islamic Movement's southern branch, also pushed for the establishment of a great Islamic caliphate that would include Israel and said all means were legitimate when it came to defending Jerusalem and Al-Aksa.[29]

While Salah is the leader of the northern branch of the Islamic Movement, regarding the Temple Mount mosques, members of the southern branch are no less extreme, and they too have promoted the notions of fighting for Al-Aksa and of "Al-Aksa is in danger." Prominent among them was Member of Knesset Abd al-Malik Dehamshe, chairman of the United Arab List in the fourteenth and fifteenth Knessets. Dehamshe, a lawyer by training, was among those issued warnings by the Or Commission and was found guilty of most of the charges against him; but because he was a Knesset member he was not penalized. The Or Commission noted in its report that "Dehamshe called again and again to be prepared to sacrifice body and soul for the defense of Al-Aksa," and that "taken as a whole, his statements make clear that defending Al-Aksa does not only refer to defending it against whoever may harm it physically, but also against a change in political arrangements." These statements were made against the background of the Camp David Conference in July 2000.[30]

In a radio interview as the conference convened, Dehamshe asserted: "As a Muslim and also as a public servant, I will not allow any harm to befall our holy of holies in this land. I think the time has come for us all to understand that this matter cannot continue in this way and we will defend it with all our might, including martyrdom." Dehamshe made similar declarations in a visit to the Temple Mount that same month and added: "We will sacrifice our souls to defend the mosque. I myself am prepared to be the first martyr to defend the Temple Mount....I am prepared and pray to be the first martyr to sacrifice his body to defend the holy of holies of Islam in Jerusalem."[31] Less than two months later, Dehamshe was again quoted as urging *jihad* by the Israeli Arab sector to prevent Israeli sovereignty over Al-Aksa.[32] Toward the end of July 2000, perhaps to underline that he meant what he said, he sent a letter to U.S. president Bill Clinton, Israeli prime minister Ehud Barak, and Palestinian Authority chairman Yasser Arafat in which he warned against infringing the sanctified status of Jerusalem. He emphasized that the Muslim and Arab masses would heed a call to die the death of the holy martyr for Al-Aksa's sake:

> If they impose it on us, and if it becomes necessary, our souls will serve as a penance, and we will be the sacrifices and the martyrs in defending our honor and in safeguarding our holy places, Al-Aksa most of all....We will not suppress the nation's anger and we will not control the popular outrage....Souls are yearning to die a martyr's death for the sake of defending Al-Aksa and blessed Jerusalem, and millions of members of the Muslim and the Arab nation will heed the call to die a death of sanctity and honor.[33]

These harsh statements were directed at the possibility that the Palestinian leadership would strike a compromise in the course of the negotiations on Jerusalem. The threat of violence indeed became a tool to achieve political goals.

A few years ago Salah crowned himself with the title "Sheikh Al-Aksa," even further upgrading the masses' total identification of him with the mosque. Any injury to him was now viewed as an injury to Al-Aksa, and during demonstrations in the Palestinian and Muslim street there were often cries of readiness to give one's life on his behalf. Salah employed tactics aimed at a total segregation of the Muslim society in Israel from the state and its institutions, and over the years he set up Muslim institutions that could form the basis for a future autonomous framework; this, in turn, would be part of his dream of a global caliphate.[34] For him, "Al-Aksa is in danger" was both a tenet in itself and an instrument toward realizing his objectives. At the beginning of 2000, Salah expressed with great precision his view of Al-Aksa and his role as its protector:

> The Al-Aksa Mosque is a Muslim, Arab, Palestinian property and no one else, whoever they may be, has any right to it; Jews especially have no right until the end of time. And whoever consents to Jews having a right to a stone there or to antiquities or to anything else, is a traitor. And it is our duty to say to that person: you are a traitor. It is treason against God, Muhammad, and the believers, against the Muslim nation, the Arab world, and the Palestinian people. It is treason against the first kibla[35] and against the Second Mosque and against the heavenward ascent of the Prophet Muhammad, and it is treason against the Al-Haram Mosque in Mecca and the Medina Mosque. It is treason against the babies of the martyrs, against Muhammad al-Dura[36] and others, and we say to whoever presumes to challenge these positions: you will not succeed. The Al-Aksa Mosque is ours

alone, and not one of you in the Jewish population has any part in it. And we still think that there is no Palestinian and no Arab and no Muslim on the face of the earth, who has in his heart a smidgen of pride, who will permit himself to give up a part, a stone, a wall, a path, a memorial rug, a dome, or a structure of the blessed Al-Aksa, from inside or outside, whether under the ground, upon the earth, or above it.[37]

Raed Salah and the Vision of a Global Islamic Caliphate: A Danger to Peace and the Western World

On June 3, 2010, Iranian television offered a live broadcast of the mass reception that Israeli Arabs gave Sheikh Raed Salah after he was released from a police investigation. Salah was arrested for participating in the Turkish flotilla that sought to breach the Israeli maritime blockade of Gaza—aboard its most problematic vessel, the *Mavi Marmara*—and this made him the hero of the day. Iran's open show of sympathy for Salah was no accident. Salah and his movement share many precepts with Iran, particularly the goal of creating a worldwide Islamic caliphate in the spirit of Muhammad. That vision is also shared, in one form or another, by the Muslim Brotherhood[1] and by the Hamas and al-Qaeda terror organizations.

Thus the dream of Salah, or "Sheikh Al-Aksa," does not focus on Jerusalem alone. Jerusalem and Al-Aksa are indeed a key element of his doctrine, but still they are only a step on a much higher ladder that leads to the objective—now feared throughout Europe—of the caliphate. If this component of Salah's worldview is still not dominant, over the years it has become increasingly central to his faith and his conduct. The "Al-Aksa is in danger" libel is not only a tool for inciting against the Jewish people and the Zionist movement, nor merely a means to upgrade the holiness of Jerusalem on the Muslim scale. In the long term this libel is also intended to help consolidate global Islam around Jerusalem as the capital of the envisaged global caliphate.

In the world according to Salah, as proclaimed from various podiums,[2] not only does Israel lack any historical or religious right to Jerusalem, and not only is the Temple a figment of the imagination. Jerusalem, in Salah's view, was a Muslim Wakf in its entirety, and must revert to exclusive Muslim rule and become the capital of the caliphate. This global entity will amend the Muslim word's fragmentation into states and constitute part of the conquest of Christianity, Europe, and the West as a whole. Salah, whose doctrine is clear-cut, speaks openly of "the global caliphate whose capital is Jerusalem," which will be "the last stage in the history of the Muslim nation until the End of Days."[3] In this era, signs of redemption will appear. The Mahdi (a designation meaning "the elected one of God," or "the guide on behalf of God"), whom Muslims regard as the redeemer of the world (comparable to the Messiah in Judaism), will emerge as well. He will arrive at the end of time, save the world from violence and injustice, and restore Islam to the original traditions of Muhammad. The era of the caliphate will also see the fulfillment of the Muslim tradition that speaks of the annihilation of Judaism. The full redemption will only occur when Muhammad's prophetic will is realized with the surrender of Christianity and the reconquest of the three cities: Jerusalem, Istanbul, and Rome, capital of Italy and seat of the Vatican.[4]

In recent years, then, Salah has been busy expanding his own and his movement's activity. He has gone from a sole focus on Jerusalem to intensive involvement with the

Palestinian issue as a whole, while indicating support for the Hamas movement and some of its main figures. In an interview with the website *Islam Online*, Salah described the broadening of his compass:

> The Muslim movement and its leadership played a prominent role on the issue of the occupied Al-Quds [Jerusalem] and Al-Aksa Mosque. This role began to expand from the local level to the general Palestinian level, and from there to the worldwide level, mainly regarding the issue of the occupied Al-Quds and Al-Aksa Mosque. This involvement has enabled the movement to forge international connections on all the matters that it concentrates on.[5]

Here Salah—possibly for the first time in public—describes the "issue of Al-Quds and Al-Aksa" not only as existing in itself but also as a means to other ends.

The trend Salah describes was tangibly manifested by his participation in the flotilla that embarked for Gaza from Turkey. Various others who were on the *Mavi Marmara* attest that Salah was a prominent figure there and made pro-*jihad* statements. In a press conference after the incident, Salah broadened his message from the national to the religious dimension, stressing the Muslims' belief in *shahada*:[6] "we say to Israel. Even if you have atomic bombs, missiles, tanks, cannons, and ground, air, and naval forces, know that it is Allah who decrees life and death. We fear no one, except the sovereign ruler of the world. That *shahada* is the faith and the duty of each of us. Each one of us must hope for it and die yearning for it."[7] Also with Salah on the ship were the chairman of the Higher Monitoring Committee of the Israeli Arabs, Muhammad Zeidan, and the head of the southern branch of the Israeli Islamic Movement, Sheikh Hamad Abu Dibas.

The vision, common to Salah and Iran, of the Islamization of the Christian continent has already begun to materialize in the Netherlands, Britain, and many other countries.[8] About fifty-four million Muslims already live in Europe today.[9] The British Centre for Social Cohesion reports that about one-third of the Muslim students in Britain favor the rule of the caliphate.[10] It is not only Salah who dreams of it. Member of Knesset Masud Ganaim, from the United Arab List–Taal party, who sat on the Central Council of the Islamic Movement and holds a BA in Middle Eastern history from the University of Haifa, proclaims a duty "to set up an Islamic caliphate and include Israel within it...since the Jews had their heyday under a caliphate of that kind." In Ganaim's view, the *nakba* (or "calamity" of Israel's creation, according to the Palestinian narrative) "stemmed from the weakness and collapse of the Muslim body, which must be rehabilitated." Ganaim took the same opportunity to express identification with the Iran-Hizbullah-Syria axis.[11]

As noted, Salah and his friends' identification with Shiite Iran is no accident given that Iran's goal is likewise a worldwide Islamic caliphate, as Iranian president Mahmoud Ahmadinejad makes clear from time to time.[12]

Meanwhile, as the worldwide-caliphate dream of Salah and his allies in Iran, Turkey, Hamas, and Hizbullah progresses, anti-Semitism rages along with occasional terror strikes in Europe and elsewhere. Already in 2000 a senior Chechen figure expressed readiness to act against the Jews. The man, a former deputy of the Chechen rebel leader Johar Dudayev, asserted that

> the goal is to stand beside our brothers in Jerusalem, and at Al-Aksa al-Sharif to the best of our ability....We have not forgotten and we will not forget our brothers at Al-Aksa. The Al-Aksa issue is the first in importance for us and for the Muslim world as a whole....The *mujahideen* have today begun, Allah be praised, practical steps for carrying out military plans against the Jews....Whoever does not...prepare himself for the liberation of Al-Aksa is distant from the Muslim nation and will die, and in his heart is something of hypocrisy....To attack the Jews everywhere. The Jews are dispersed and visible, Allah be praised, and it is possible to carry out military actions against them.[13]

Hamas, some of whose positions Sheikh Salah openly supports, is a terrorist organization in every regard. The Islamic Movement in Umm al-Fahm, however, is linked to Hamas in a way that is not only ideological. In 2008, the Israel Police and the Shin Bet closed the offices of the Al-Aksa Institute in Umm al-Fahm after its cooperation with Hamas headquarters in Jerusalem was uncovered. This cooperation, as the Shin Bet made clear, was funded by (among others) the Coalition of Justice—a worldwide roof organization of extremist Muslim foundations that was operated by Hamas. Already in 2002 Israel had declared it illicit.[14]

A Hamas greeting card illustrating the purported Jewish-Israeli threat to the Dome of the Rock. Found in a mosque by the IDF during Operation Defensive Shield, 2002. (Tsvika Israeli, Government Press Office)

Hamas, like Salah, makes frequent use of the "Al-Aksa is in danger" libel. Like him, too, Hamas speaks of a Muslim revolution that will bring about Islam's conquest of the globe. A typical example is a statement by Yunis al-Astal, a representative of Hamas on the Palestinian Authority's Legislative Council, who warned in March 2008 of Zionist plans to murder "Sheikh Al-Aksa Raed Salah"—plans motivated, in al-Astal's telling, by Salah's repeated warnings of a Zionist plot to destroy the Al-Aksa Mosque.[15] A month later al-Astal broadened his purview and declared that Islam would soon conquer Rome, "capital of the Catholics or the Crusaders," just as it had once conquered Constantinople, and from there it would proceed to take over the two Americas as well as Eastern Europe.[16]

Along with the Muslim demographic threat to Europe comes a constant threat of terror. Shiraz Maher, a young Briton of Pakistani extraction who for three years was among the leadership of an organization that supports and preaches international terror, described in September 2010 how he advocated terror, justified the actions of Hamas, favored blowing up buses and attacking children, and was haunted for years by the call of his organization's leaders: "You, the children of Saladin, must liberate Al-Aksa at any price." "The organization's principles, which posit that democracy is not compatible with Islam, the State of Israel must be obliterated, and the laws of *sharia* must be imposed, making use of violence, all over the world—were my sustenance," Maher acknowledged in May 2010 in a lecture at the International Institute for Counter-Terrorism of the Interdisciplinary Center in Herzliya, Israel.[17]

Thus, Hamas, Iran, Salah and his movement, and any other actor promoting the idea of a global Islamic caliphate are all part of the same phenomenon. Promoting the idea by violent means is also favored, as noted, by al-Qaeda as well as Hizbullah, which aspires to export the Muslim revolution all over the world and whose leader, Hassan Nasrallah, also chimes in that "Israel is seeking to destroy the Al-Aksa Mosque."[18]

Sheikh Akrama Sabri, the former mufti of Jerusalem who was appointed to his post by the Palestinian Authority, is also among the leading disseminators of the "Al-Aksa is in danger" libel. A few weeks before the September 11 attack, the sheikh gave a speech in which he implored: "Allah, bring destruction on the United States, on those who help it and all who cooperate with it." Sabri also called for the annihilation of Great Britain.[19]

Yet another "agent" that spreads the "Al-Aksa is in danger" libel among the Muslim masses is the Islamic Liberation Party (Hizb ut-Tahrir), whose founder, Sheikh Taqi al-Din al-Nabhani, was a protégé of the Muslim Brotherhood. Hizb ut-Tahrir is active in the Palestinian Authority, eastern Jerusalem, and in clandestine cells in Europe. This movement, too, includes the dream of the caliphate in its worldview. In June 2008, one of its senior figures, Khaled Said, presented his organization's main precepts: faith, the caliphate, and *jihad*.[20] The movement has held several rallies on the Temple Mount, from which it openly called for the global caliphate.[21] Some Arab and European countries have declared Hizb ut-Tahrir illegal.[22] In Germany, for instance, the organization was outlawed after it emerged that the "brain" behind the September 11 attack, Mohammed Atta, was influenced by its ideology. Hizb ut-Tahrir believes that the creation of a caliphate is a precondition for the declaration of *jihad*, and Western observers consider it an organization that lays the groundwork for al-Qaeda and even is a "production line for terrorists."[23]

The "Al-Aksa is in danger" libel, then, is not separate from the vision of a global Islamic caliphate and the export of Islam throughout the world. The libel is a tool in the hands of its disseminators to focus world attention on Jerusalem, which, according to Salah and some of his partners in the idea, is destined to be the caliphate's capital.

Terror from the Temple Mount Mosques

Given the "Al Aksa is in danger" libel, the calls to come and defend the mosques even if it means sacrificing one's life and shedding blood, and the violent language Muslim clerics have used within and outside the Temple Mount to radicalize their message, it comes as no surprise that sometimes the Temple Mount mosques are used for purposes of terror. Using the mount and its mosques as a terror base is legitimized by the notion that this base is "threatened" by the "enemies of Islam." Since attacking the enemies of Islam is legitimate, so is planning attacks from the precincts of "threatened" and "endangered" Al-Aksa.

It comes as no surprise, too, that senior Muslim clerics (Sunni and Shiite), most of all the Sunni sheikh Yusuf al-Qaradawi and the Shiite Ayatollah Khomeini, have often affirmed the legitimacy of using mosques for military purposes and for terror against the enemies of Islam in the context of *jihad* (holy war).[1] Qaradawi, the spiritual patron of the Muslim Brotherhood whose views sit comfortably with Hamas, has spoken in the past of the imminent conquest of Europe.[2] He has pointed out that, since the earliest days of Islam, the mosque has played an important role in encouraging Muslims to embark on *jihad* and resistance against enemies of the Muslim community, those seeking to invade and rule it. Khomeini, for his part, stated that "the mosque is a fortress of the great *jihad*," a place for warfare against Satan and the despots.[3] Experts at Israel's Meir Amit Intelligence and Terrorism Information Center note that this outlook is based on the *hadith* that the Prophet Muhammad himself used the mosque for both military and political ends, beyond its function as a house of prayer for the believers.[4]

Like the "Al-Aksa is in danger" libel itself, the use of the Temple Mount compound for terror purposes began in the period of the grand mufti Haj Amin al-Husseini, who was a pioneer in this regard as well. The mufti, who took part in stoking the Great Arab Revolt against the British of 1936-1939, was removed by the British from all his posts. When they tried to arrest him he found refuge in the Temple Mount mosques, and in October 1937 succeeded to escape from Palestine. As Dr. Dotan Goren of Bar-Ilan University notes, in this period the mosques served as a hiding place for weapons and tools of sabotage, and the Temple Mount compound became a haven for members of the Arab gangs that took part in the Great Arab Revolt. Indeed, in July 1938 a large quantity of weapons was found beside the Dome of the Rock, concealed within building materials meant for renovations at the site. The weapons included bombs, bullets, a rifle, and more.[5]

In those days hundreds of members of Arab terrorist gangs were able to infiltrate the Old City of Jerusalem. The British, in a military operation, entered the Old City and drove the gang members onto the Temple Mount. Attempting to prove that no weapons were hidden there, the Wakf invited the British to enter the mount—where they found, near the mosque, "a number of boxes that had been emptied of hand grenades."[6]

The Temple Mount was likewise used for military purposes during the War of Independence. A report from November 1947[7] reveals that there was an Arab headquarters on the mount from which weapons were distributed. A guard was stationed at the entrance to the room where the weapons were stashed, and every Arab who came to obtain weapons paid a set fee or brought a guarantor of payment.[8]

During the First and Second Intifadas, too, the Temple Mount was used to incite riots and insurrection. Eventually it became clear that several Palestinian terrorist gangs had chosen the Temple Mount plaza as a regular meeting place. Gang members held parleys mainly during prayer hours, using the site's sacredness for cover to plan operations.

On October 15, 1986, the most notable of these gangs carried out a grenade attack against Israeli recruits of the Givati Brigade at their swearing-in ceremony at the Western Wall. Dov Porat, the father of a soldier, was killed; sixty-nine others, including soldiers and their family members, were injured. The terrorists left leaflets in the vicinity inscribed by "the members of the Temple Mount gang, a company of the Muslim sacred guard in Palestine." The text of the leaflets was religious, mainly verses from the Koran.[9] Within a short time the Shin Bet arrested the brothers Nasser and Tarek Halisi from Silwan village, which borders the scene of the attack. Their interrogation revealed that they were recruited by the PLO in Jordan in a religious context, and that the Temple Mount mosques were among the gang's meeting places.[10]

The gang that kidnapped and murdered border policeman Nissim Toledano in December 1992 and traffic policemen Daniel Hazut and Mordechai Yisrael in March 1993 also used the Temple Mount and its mosques to plan their acts of terror. The gang members, who belonged to Hamas, each received three life sentences. Before he was sentenced, gang leader Mahmoud Issa told the judges: "The Koran obligates us to *jihad*. We, the Izzadin al-Kassam gang, carried out all the *jihad* operations in defense of the Koran. We are members of the people whose land was conquered and whose honor was humiliated...we could not stay quiet."[11]

During the First Intifada in 1988, the preachers in their Friday sermons on the Temple Mount sometimes included passages from leaflets published by the United National Headquarters. On July 3 of that year, the preacher quoted from Announcement No. 22 on the "Blessed Holiday of the Sacrifice": "The United National Headquarters praises the strike forces for their active role against the occupation forces, mechanisms, and ministries and against those who deviate from the will of the people." Announcement No. 21, published a short time earlier, was called the "Blessed Al-Aksa Mosque Announcement." It designated August 7 of that year as "Al-Aksa Day," a "special day of escalation, in which the public will take part in all the mass activities to defend Al-Aksa; a day in which the strike forces will inflict blows on the enemy forces and the settler herds."[12]

In April 1993, the Temple Mount mosques served as a meeting place where initial contacts were made between Fatah activists and Hamas and Islamic Jihad activists, aimed at strengthening the operational links between them. A month earlier Israel had expelled four hundred Hamas men to Lebanon after a severe wave of terror attacks by the organization. Also in those years, a ceremonial event was held on the Temple Mount in which a "Palestinian Declaration of Independence" was read out.[13] On the mount itself in 1995, Hassan Ariba of Abu Dis village that borders Jerusalem stabbed Israeli police officer Yitzchak Limai. Ariba fell upon Limai with cries of "Allah Akbar" and severely wounded him.[14]

During June and July 2008, Israeli security services arrested six Arab residents of eastern Jerusalem, some of them students at the Hebrew University, who were members of an extremist Muslim group that held meetings at the Al-Aksa Mosque. There they made plans to set up an al-Qaeda infrastructure and perpetrate terror attacks in Israel. One had looked into the possibility of shooting down the helicopter of U.S. president George Bush during his January 2008 visit to Jerusalem. The group's leader was Yusef Sumarin, a former security prisoner who had been freed a short time earlier.[15]

Likewise, those who hatched the plot to fire a missile at Teddy Stadium in Jerusalem in the spring of 2010, during a soccer game when crowds of people would be there, were tied to the Temple Mount. According to the charge sheet against Bassam al-Omri (convicted) and Moussa Hamada (his trial was still in progress at this writing), the two worked as Hamas representatives at the Al-Aksa Mosque for three years.[16] Their employer, Majid Jubeh, admitted in the framework of a plea bargain that he was in charge of a Hamas gang that worked for the Al-Aksa Committee on the mount.[17] Jubeh was sentenced to two years in prison. And on August 22, 2011, a severe attack in Jerusalem was prevented when Sayid Qawasma, a suicide terrorist who planned to blow himself up in the Pisgat Zeev neighborhood, was caught while hiding on the mount near the Al-Aksa Mosque.[18]

There is good reason to believe that the terror gangs' use of the Temple Mount mosques and plazas to plan attacks was influenced by the atmosphere on the mount itself. Without the freedom to incite that, in effect, the Israeli authorities have granted to the various preachers and sermonizers, it is doubtful whether young Muslims would allow themselves—using the mosques as protection—to take the further step into actual violence. Matters came to a head in May 2011 after U.S. commando forces killed the arch-terrorist who was behind the Twin Towers attacks, Al-Qaeda chief Osama Bin Laden. "Western dogs," intoned the preacher at the Al-Aksa Mosque a few hours later,

> have murdered a lion of the lions of Islam. The West today rejoiced over the killing of a lion of the lions of Islam....You [Obama] said that you personally gave the order to kill the Muslims. Know well, soon you will hang on a rope along

with little Bush. From here, from the Al-Aksa Mosque, from the place of the next Islamic caliphate, we say to them: the dogs will not rejoice much longer over the killing of the lions.

Hours after U.S. commandos killed Osama Bin Laden, the preacher at the Al-Aksa Mosque intoned: "You [Obama] said that you personally gave the order to kill the Muslims. Know well, soon you will hang on a rope along with little Bush."

Until the First Intifada broke out, for the most part Israeli and Jordanian influences moderated the tenor of the sermons delivered in the mosques each Friday. But when the intifada erupted, the rules of the game on the Temple Mount changed and the oracles of religion only looked for excuses to inflame their followers. The change was particularly apparent in statements about the intifada by the then mufti Saad al-Din al-Alami to the PLO's official organ *Filastin al-Thawra*.

Al-Alami, chairman of the Supreme Muslim Council, swore in the interview to continue the uprising and framed it as a question of life and death for the residents. His support for the armed struggle was evident in a request he directed to certain Arab elements to obtain weapons rather than money, and in his appeal to the Arab peoples to pressure their governments to go to war against Israel. Al-Alami also told baseless atrocity stories: "The eyes of three Gaza youths were gouged out by IDF soldiers, after which they shot them." He called the Israeli prisons "death camps," and told of a "special torture implement that extracts the liquid from the eye, an implement now used in the Israeli prisons." This, he explained, accounted for the rise in blindness cases in the territories.[19]

So long as Jordan ruled the Temple Mount (1948-1967), incitement of this kind was met by tough measures and substantial punishment by the authorities. The Israeli leadership, however, rejected a recommendation by security circles to expel al-Alami. The mayor of Jerusalem at the time, Teddy Kollek, told al-Alami in a reproachful letter that his statements were "distant from reality and include imaginary descriptions whose aim is to incite and damage the fabric of relations between the two peoples, Jewish and Arab." Al-Alami felt sufficiently sure of himself to send Kollek a reply in which he did not retract his claims.[20]

Israel's treatment of Sheikh al-Alami, who indeed favored an armed struggle against Israel, was symptomatic of the Israeli government's behavior in general toward the senior religious figures on the Temple Mount. It was mainly marked by profound deference to the religious autonomy that had been granted them. In the Jordanian period, the authorities did not hesitate to impose strict limitations on the Muslim clerics of the mount. On the orders of the king and his emissaries, before presenting their sermons the *khatib*s (preachers) had to submit a copy to the local Wakf administration. Sermons that contradicted the official line usually drew a fine and sometimes even imprisonment. The Jordanian authorities also imposed stiff terms on *khatib*s who failed to bless the king at the end of the Friday sermon; in Muslim history, omitting the blessing of the ruler was considered a clear sign of disloyalty to him.[21]

In files of the Jordanian internal security service that fell into Israeli hands during the Six-Day War, the Israeli authorities found abundant evidence of the Jordanian regime's harsh line toward members of the religious establishment; in comparison, the Israeli authorities treated them with kid gloves.

The Palestinian Authority—both in the Arafat and Mahmoud Abbas (Abu Mazen) periods—also forbade West Bank preachers from giving sermons of a political nature, requiring them to submit the contents of their sermons for prior approval, and sometimes dismissing or even arresting preachers who are identified with Hamas.[22] Sheikh Jamal Muhammad Ahmed Bawatba, minister for Wakf and religious affairs in the government of Salam Fayyad, even hinted in 2009 that preachers would be dismissed "who do not adhere to the message of the mosque, and to the message of the [Wakf] ministry." He added: "Recently a number of preachers and instructors in the mosques have negatively exploited the freedom that is given them....Someone who wants fame and election propaganda should go to the radio and TV stations."[23] An article by journalist Ali Waked describes the struggle the PA wages against Hamas activity in the mosques. Waked notes the "reeducation" of preachers, and the expulsion from West Bank mosques of tens (according to other sources, hundreds) of Hamas-affiliated imams. A preacher at a Ramallah-area mosque told Waked: "We occasionally receive a notice from the Religious Affairs Ministry specifying the subject of the sermon for the week, and we are forbidden to deviate from that subject....We stopped dealing with politics a long time ago."[24]

In the Arab and Muslim world, the use of mosques for military and political purposes prompts much harsher responses. After September 11, 2001, the Saudi authorities took action against mosques where members of al-Qaeda and other Muslim terror groups had taken refuge.[25] In July 2007, the main mosque of Islamabad, Pakistan, the "Red Mosque," became a center of terror and incitement against the Muslim regime there, and the Pakistani army broke into it. About a hundred supporters of extremist Islam in Pakistan were killed in the operation including Abd al-Aziz Ayazi, deputy of the imam of the mosque. The Pakistani move was a response to mass-casualty terror attacks perpetrated by supporters of Ayazi.[26] In Egypt as well, the authorities acted against mosques that were centers of incitement and terror. They based themselves on a ruling by Muhammad al-Tantawi, sheikh of Al-Azhar University and considered a senior religious authority in the Sunni Muslim world. In July 2007, the website of the Muslim Brotherhood in Egypt noted that the sheikh had affirmed: "A state has the full right to attack mosques, seal them and even destroy them in the interest of maintaining state security."[27]

Some may claim that what is permitted for a Muslim government and a non-Muslim one in countering incitement and terror from mosques is not the same. Israel, however, has behaved more mildly in this regard than even Western countries such as Britain, Germany, Italy, or Spain, which have not hesitated to take measures against mosques and religious figures when confronted with incitement and/or terror.[28]

Despite the severe incitement voiced by Temple Mount clerics over the years and particularly the "Al-Aksa is in danger" libel, Israel is very wary about taking the sorts of measures that Muslim and other Western countries take. Israel has often, however, set age limits for those who come to pray on the mount, based on intelligence information about likely disturbances. Such outbreaks have occurred periodically in recent years, reaching a peak with the throwing of stones, cinder blocks, and building materials at Jewish worshippers in the Western Wall plaza below the mount. This happened, for example, on September 29, 2000, when an incited mass threw stones—marshaled beforehand—at worshippers at the wall. It occurred in the presence of Palestinian Authority religious officials and security men, whom Israel had allowed to be there in the hope that this might preserve calm. Stones had also been thrown at worshippers at the wall during the First Intifada (for example, in April 1989 and in October 1990).[29]

Israel's liberal approach to the Temple Mount, and its leaders' perplexity in the face of the incitement and violence that issue from there, were already evident years ago in a statement by Teddy Kollek who served as mayor of Jerusalem for almost three decades (1965-1993). Kollek wrote a biting but also somewhat desperate letter to the then director-general of the Wakf, Sheikh Abd al-Azim Salhub. Kollek reminded him that he personally, along with the City of Jerusalem, was among those who supported the post-Six-Day War decision to leave the mount in the hands of the leaders of the Muslim religion. "This policy," Kollek noted,

> stipulated a tolerant approach that enables each of the religions to run its religious affairs independently and without interference....In the past we have seen infractions of the public order of different magnitudes. In many cases we acted with restraint and even persuaded others to show tolerance. However, what has happened [Kollek referred to the throwing of stones at Jewish worshippers at the Western Wall in April 1989] violates all the rules of the game that were in place until today.... Throughout the years I have preached tolerance and understanding between the religions and between the peoples, because I believe in this. But I do not consider it acceptable that a small group, wild and irresponsible, should prevent members of the other religion from freely practicing their religion. Tolerance has to run both ways. We cannot fight for the Muslims' right to manage their

In times of tension the Muslim worshippers at Al-Aksa have attacked the worshippers at the Western Wall, hurling stones at them as here in the mid-'90s. (Avi Ochayon, Government Press Office)

The Western Wall plaza strewn with stones hurled from the Temple Mount after the Jewish worshippers were evacuated from the plaza, 1994. (Avi Ochayon, Government Press Office)

affairs on the Temple Mount freely and without external interference, while you pay us back with a lack of the most minimal, elementary maintenance of control on the mount....I demand that you exercise the powers that were granted you to preserve law and order on the Temple Mount. I am profoundly apprehensive that if you are unable to do so, and if Jewish worshippers cannot pray at the Western Wall without harassment, the State of Israel will of course find a way to ensure freedom of religion at the holy places.[30]

In retrospect, Kollek's letter indeed appears unique but also naïve. Kollek reproached the Wakf leadership for failing to put a lid on the violence while ignoring the fact that some of that very leadership was taking part, actively or passively, in that very violence. The main players on the Temple Mount—Jordan, the PLO, the Palestinian Authority, Hamas, and the Israeli Islamic Movement—have turned the mount, essentially a religious site, into a political ax to grind, and the libelous and inflammatory cry of "Al-Aksa is in danger" has served them more than any other tool.

The Archeological Digs: Near the Temple Mount and Not Under It

The archeological digs Israel has conducted over the years *near* the Temple Mount are a laudable scientific and cultural endeavor. Publication of the results has enabled all lovers of culture, science, and religion, and the members of all the communities—Jews, Christians, and Muslims—to identify the relics of their past that are immersed in the soil of Jerusalem, to learn about them and exult in them, deepening their bond to that past. But it is natural that the State of Israel, the state of the Jewish people who returned to Jerusalem and Zion after two thousand years in exile, did not remain indifferent to findings from the earlier epochs which corresponded with Jewish historical sources and sacred writings. Discoveries and publications about the Jewish people's ancient past in Jerusalem won greater public attention. At the same time, the archeologists did not disdain periods when other peoples and religions were present in Jerusalem. They revealed, documented, and published these findings meticulously, in keeping with scientific standards.

The propagators of the "Al-Aksa is in danger" libel have ignored this. One of their regular rituals since the unification of Jerusalem in 1967 has centered on the archeological digs surrounding the Temple Mount: each time Israel has dug near the mount or at the foot of its walls, the cry of "Al-Aksa is in danger" has rung out in response.

This chapter focuses on several sites near the Temple Mount where Israel has carried out archeological digs. Regarding every one of these sites it has been charged that the work there endangers Al-Aksa. In each case the charge goes hand in hand with severe incitement and sometimes also violence. The incitement and the charges fall on attentive ears even though in each and every case the charge is without foundation.

The archeological digs Israel has conducted over the years near the Temple Mount are a laudable scientific and cultural endeavor. Every one has been said to endanger Al-Aksa, although in every case the charge is without foundation.

The study of the history of Jerusalem, which has fascinated generations of historians and researchers, has suffered from one glaring lack—scientific excavations or archeological discoveries on the Temple Mount itself. Although such discoveries could have been the crowning glory of Temple Mount researchers, until 1967 almost no excavations were done at the site. Up to the mid-nineteenth century the Muslim authorities forbade archeologists, researchers, scientists, religious representatives, and those of various worldviews and nations to even enter the mount, let alone dig there, and even posed obstacles to researching its nearby surroundings. When Kaiser Wilhelm, who toured the Dome of the Rock in 1898, told his hosts that "it is a pity that excavations are not being carried out at this important site," the kadi accompanying him looked heavenward and said, "A man should direct his eyes and his thoughts upward, at the skies, instead of downward to the depths."[1] When Montagu Brownlow Parker, a British adventurer who headed a group that stole into the mount in 1911, carried out a secret excavation in the vicinity of Al-Aksa and the Dome of the Rock over several nights, the Wakf quickly found out. Parker and his group, who were discovered while digging beneath the Drinking Stone (or rock of Mount Moriah) in the hope of finding the treasures of the Temple there, hurriedly escaped to a yacht that awaited them at Jaffa port and returned to Europe.[2]

This policy of the Wakf and the Muslim clerics did not change after the Six-Day War; indeed, it was reinforced. In the background lurked the fear (intensified by the Crusader history) that the European powers would gain access to the Temple Mount; but the main, undisguised fear was that excavations in the general vicinity and on the mount in particular would disclose relics of the Jewish presence on the mount from First and Second Temple days, which might contradict religious suppositions rooted in the Islamic outlook.[3] Moreover, archeological discoveries that would yield further evidence of the Temples' existence could, from the Muslim standpoint, topple the whole elaborate edifice of denial of the Jewish link to the place, an edifice in which the "Al-Aksa is in danger" libel played an important role. Even when archeological relics from various periods were discovered accidentally during development and renovation work on the mount, the Wakf hastened to hush up the find and prevent the dig from going further.[4]

Except for a single case, Israel honored the Muslim precepts and never excavated under the Temple Mount, only along its walls or at some distance from them. The thousands of publications claiming Israel was digging under the mosques were, then, mendacious. Only in 1981 did an official state functionary take his own initiative and empty the mud and water in an existing tunnel that led eastward from the Western Wall under the Temple Mount compound. The rabbi of the Western Wall and the holy places, Rabbi Yehuda Meir Getz, who dreamed of discovering the Temple implements, removed a blockage of the Second Temple-era gate that researchers call either Cistern 30 or Warren's Gate. Without the authorization or knowledge of the government, he began hauling out large quantities of mud and water from the entry tunnel that extends about 30 meters from Warren's Gate under the Temple Mount. Getz was not scheming to bring down the mosques. He indeed was among those rabbis who forbade entering the mount on Halakhic (Jewish law) grounds. Nevertheless, when his action came to light, Prime Minister Menachem Begin and Police Minister Dr. Yosef Burg ordered that the gate be sealed and even had a concrete cover added.[5]

Throughout the 44 years of Israeli rule over united Jerusalem and its holy places, Israel has uncovered the entire extent—under the ground surface—of the Western Wall, at the foot of which Jews have prayed for centuries. The total length of the wall is 488 meters. The first 81 meters on the southern side (including the earthen ramp leading

Facing the "Holy of Holies" (the site of the Jewish Temple) in the Western Wall Tunnel. On the right: the concrete blockage from 1981. The gate was sealed at the order of then-prime minister Menachem Begin to prevent passage under the Temple Mount. (courtesy of the Western Wall Heritage Foundation)

to the Mughrabi Gate) were excavated and researched after the Six-Day War by archeologists Benjamin Mazar and Meir Ben-Dov, and today are an archeological tourist site and not a prayer plaza.[6] The next 57 meters are the open prayer plaza that the State of Israel prepared after the Six-Day War. The remaining 350 meters of the Western Wall, northward from that point, were excavated by the Religious Affairs Ministry beneath the streets and houses of the Old City, in the area known as the Western Wall Tunnel. In addition, Israel unearthed and also cleaned out the Hasmonean Channel, an ancient aqueduct from Second Temple days (or the end of First Temple days) that extends along the length of the Western Wall in a northward direction, but not under the Temple Mount.

Israel has excavated the City of David south of the Temple Mount; the digs there are 150 to 500 meters from the mount. Israeli archeologists have also dug at the foot of the Southern Wall of the mount, on Haggai Street in the Muslim Quarter of the Old City, at the Western Wall plaza, and under the ramp that led to the Mughrabi Gate, before natural erosion caused its collapse in February 2004. The Israel Antiquities Authority has carried out rescue digs in many other parts of the Old City of Jerusalem and its environs, in keeping with Israeli law mandating rescue digs of this kind at any construction site, and particularly in areas with an archeological potential such as Jerusalem and its Old City.

Such activity was conducted, for example, in the vicinity of Jaffa Gate, where in February 2010 a main thoroughfare was discovered of Byzantine-era Jerusalem about 1500 years ago. This finding aroused great excitement since it confirmed the authenticity of the Madaba Map, an ancient mosaic map from the sixth century CE that was discovered in a church in Jordan and portrayed the Land of Israel in the Byzantine era. The urgent need to strengthen the foundations of structures in the Old City led to rescue digs and to findings that included a trove of earthenware, weights, and coins from various periods.[7] Also discovered was the upper aqueduct of Jerusalem from the Roman period, about 1800 years old.[8] In October 2010, the need to build a *mikveh* (Jewish ritual bath) in the Jewish Quarter of the Old City led to rescue digs that revealed a bathing pool, part of a Roman bathhouse from the second-third centuries CE. Tiles of the bathhouse still bore the seal of Fretensis, the Tenth Roman Legion.

This finding was significant because until then, despite extensive digs in the Jewish Quarter, not a single structure of the Roman Legion had been discovered there. The new finding attested that Aelia Capitolina, the Roman city established after the destruction of Jerusalem, occupied a wider area than was previously thought.[9]

Over the years numerous rescue digs have been carried out in many other locations in Jerusalem, which is a dynamic and developing city, and have turned up interesting findings from various periods. From 2005 to 2009, remnants were discovered of buildings from various eras including the First Temple period in the western part of the Western Wall plaza, about a hundred meters west of the Temple Mount. These excavations were conducted prior to the construction of a large educational center that the Western Wall Heritage Foundation wants to build there. The digs also unearthed remnants of an impressive Roman street as well as five Hebrew seals. On one of the seals the name of its owner, Hagav, was preserved, along with a fine ornament in an Assyrian style of a soldier carrying a bow. The other seals also bear the Hebrew names of their owners, and also found near them was a profusion of earthenware with handles of jugs carrying impressions that are known in the research as "impressions of the king," from the days of King Hezekiah of Judah (eighth century BCE).[10] This cultural wealth that the soil of Jerusalem harbored within it did not persuade the Muslims. Virtually any blow of an Israeli archeologist's trowel in the vicinity of the Old City and near the Temple Mount sparks cries of "Al-Aksa is in danger!" This has been a fraudulent campaign, deliberately timed and focused especially on certain sites.

Eight Excavation Sites—Eight Test Cases

9.1 The Excavations at the Foot of the Southern Wall (1968-1978)

Background: Prof. Benjamin Mazar, the first Israeli archeologist to dig at the foot of the Southern Wall after the Six-Day War, first requested to dig at the Western Wall but was turned down by the then religious affairs minister, Dr. Zerah Warhaftig, and the Chief Rabbinate. These regarded the Western Wall as a place of prayer only. Mazar was left with the Southern Wall, and on February 28, 1968, he and his assistant Meir Ben-Dov launched the excavations there, licensed by the Israel Antiquities Authority. The Society for the Study of the Land of Israel and Its Antiquities, the National Academy of Sciences, the National Parks Authority, and the Hebrew University gave the dig their sponsorship, and it also won the support of then-Jerusalem Mayor Teddy Kollek.[11]

The Muslims' Charges: During the 1970s and 1980s, Jordan and other Arab countries passed countless resolutions in international forums condemning Israel for archeological digs carried out at the foot of the Southern Wall. The Muslims charged that the digs penetrated under the mosques' foundations and were threatening the wall's stability. UN institutions were flooded with complaints that Israel was changing the Muslim historical, cultural, and religious nature of eastern Jerusalem.

The Answer to the Charges: In fact, these digs unearthed impressive relics of the Muslim presence in Jerusalem. The excavation was conducted in the vicinity of the Southern Wall, southward in the direction of the Old City walls, and never extended northward to under the Temple Mount compound. At least in one case, in the area of the Hulda Gates where the excavators discovered an underground passage from the area of the digs to the surface of the Temple Mount compound, Israel had the passage blocked in coordination with the Wakf.[12]

The excavation was conducted in the vicinity of the Southern Wall, southward, and never extended northward to under the Temple Mount compound.

In March 1983, police arrested four yeshiva students carrying excavation trowels at the site of the archeological digs at the foot of the Southern Wall, on suspicion that they planned to infiltrate the Temple Mount through an underground passage. Their comrades in the nearby Jewish Quarter were arrested as well. They were tried but exonerated. Although this incident is not directly connected to archeological digs, it occurred in the vicinity of an excavation site and shows how determined Israel was to prevent the digs' spillover into the Temple Mount compound, or digging of any other kind under the compound.[13]

The stability of the Southern Wall was weakened many years later when the Wakf and the Israeli Islamic Movement carried out operations at the southeastern corner of the Temple Mount compound whose aim was to convert the underground recess known as Solomon's Stables into a mosque (see Chapter 10).

Cautionary and Safety Measures Taken by Israel: The excavation was overseen by a safety committee made up of representatives of the City of Jerusalem, the Defense Ministry, the Labor Ministry, and the archeological team. Later the safety supervision was put in the hands of a team of professionals, including experts from the Technion in Haifa. In line with an appraisal by Technion experts, heavy security beams were emplaced within the dig at the foot of the Southern Wall to reinforce the wall's stability during the work.[14]

Informal Muslim Attitudes: The heads of the Wakf and the Supreme Muslim Council visited the site several times and received professional briefings from Mazar and Ben-Dov, the heads of the archeological team that excavated the site. Following a conversation between Ben-Dov and Anwar Nusseibeh, governor of the Jerusalem district and a minister in the Jordanian government while it ruled Jerusalem, Nusseibeh's son, Sari Nusseibeh, came to the site and worked there shoulder to shoulder with the Jewish excavators. He was especially intrigued by the findings from the Umayyad period, and under their impact began to study Muslim philosophy and history.[15] In one of the visits to the place, the mufti Halami al-Muhtaseb and Wakf secretary Ghassan Tahboub waxed enthusiastic over the findings and the team's work.[16] One Muslim visitor who requested anonymity was so impressed by what he saw that he told a friend in an unhindered conversation: "What is all this nonsense coming from Jordan about the digs destroying the mosque? We can see with our own eyes that this admirable excavation is unearthing finds from the Islamic period. They're really gems." The director of the Jordanian Antiquities Department, Rafik Dajani, was also favorably impressed by the Israeli endeavor and said so openly. The Jordanian authorities retaliated by firing him from his post.[17]

One Muslim visitor told a friend: "What is all this nonsense coming from Jordan about the digs destroying the mosque? We can see with our own eyes that this admirable excavation is unearthing finds from the Islamic period. They're really gems."

Main Archeological Findings:[18] At the convergence of the walls (Southern and Western), a paved road was found that extends both northward and southward that was Jerusalem's main thoroughfare in late Second Temple days. Here a stone was discovered, which had fallen from above at the southwestern corner of the Temple Mount, bearing a broken inscription in Hebrew that can be rendered as: "The shofar blast di...," which apparently can be completed as "The shofar blast divides between the sacred and the

Volunteers uncover the hidden treasures of Jerusalem at the foot of the Southern Wall, immediately after the Six-Day War. The heads of the Supreme Muslim Council visited the spot and expressed enthusiasm, but in public they leveled charges. (Fritz Cohen, Government Press Office)

profane," as appears in written sources including Josephus' *The Jewish War*.[19] The stone seems to have marked the spot where the Temple Mount priests stood when they blew the trumpets to proclaim the entry and departure of the Sabbath.

In the area from the Southern Wall to the Old City walls, and also to the west of the southern part of the Western Wall, four imposing palaces were discovered from the Umayyad period, the beginning of Muslim rule in Jerusalem.[20] Carved onto the walls of the rooms were pairs of pillars that supported stone arches, extending for the full length of each room, on which the ceiling was laid. In the basement rooms that were excavated at the southwestern corner of one of the palaces was found, among other things, a pillar that had been taken from somewhere else, which bore an engraved inscription of the Tenth Roman Legion. The pillar also bore a Latin inscription with the names of the Roman Caesars Vespasian and Titus, who waged the war to suppress the Great Revolt of the Jews (66-70 CE).

Arab workers at the excavations of the Southern Wall. (Ya'acov Sa'ar, Government Press Office)

Another era is represented by a building from the Middle Ages that abutted the Southern Wall and the Al-Aksa Mosque. Additional structures from the Byzantine period, including rooms, courtyards, and recesses carved in rock, were preserved under the foundations and floors of the Umayyad palaces.

One of the spectacular findings was the rediscovery of the Hulda Gates, the two main entrance gates to the Temple Mount in the Second Temple period at the Southern Wall, and the giant staircase that leads to them. The western Hulda Gate, known as the Double Gate, is situated below the Al-Aksa Mosque and at present is closed off like its neighbor, the eastern Hulda Gate. Also discovered nearby was a network of *mikveh*s which served the Jews who ascended the mount in Second Temple times. Many other findings, from First Temple days to the Ottoman era, were made at the location including lintels with crosses from the Byzantine period, on which seven-branched menorahs were painted in red during the Persian conquest or the early Umayyad era.

9.2 The Excavations at the Foot of the Western Wall (1968-1978)

Background: Two months after the archeological digs at the foot of the Western Wall began, they also reached the southern end of this wall. This occurred to the distress of the Religious Affairs Ministry and the chief rabbis, who had hoped to widen the prayer plaza in this area as well. Over the years, however, the rabbinical establishment came to accept this reality and a division was made: the area to the south of the Mughrabi Gate, along the Western Wall, became a place for archeological excavation, while the area along the Western Wall to the north of the Mughrabi Gate was designated for prayer.

The Muslims' Charges: The excavations "Judaize" the Western Wall, which is actually part of the Al-Aksa compound and the wall to which Muhammad tethered Al-Buraq in the midst of his Night Journey from Mecca to Jerusalem. The excavations seek to undermine the Western Wall and the stability of the Temple Mount compound with the aim of toppling the mosques.

The Answer to the Charges: The Israeli authorities could not possibly seek to damage the Western Wall, to which the Jewish religion attributes special holiness and about which the Midrash says: "The Shekhinah has never departed from the Western Wall."[21] When in 1972 some holes were mistakenly drilled in the "Little Western Wall," the northward extension of the Western Wall, religious and haredi Jewry were in an uproar and the State of Israel set up an investigatory commission to find out how such a thing could have happened.[22] This incident, seemingly minor, illustrates how divorced from reality is the Muslim charge that Israel seeks to topple the Western Wall and subsequently the mosques as well. Visits and inspections at the site in the 1980s and 1990s by UNESCO envoy Prof. Raymond Lamar found no basis for the charge that the excavations were harming the stability of the mount.

Cautionary and Safety Measures Taken by Israel: The digs at the foot of the Western Wall were in fact carried out concurrently with those at the foot of the Southern Wall, and the former, too, were accompanied by a safety committee composed of representatives of the City of Jerusalem, the Defense Ministry, the Labor Ministry, and the archeological team. Later as well, safety supervision was entrusted to a team of professionals, including Technion experts. The excavations were conducted solely at the foot of the Western Wall and did not deviate eastward under the Temple Mount compound.

Informal Muslim Attitudes: In this case, too, the heads of the Wakf and the Supreme Muslim Council visited several times and heard professional explanations from the heads of the archeological team, Mazar and Ben-Dov. The visitors requested that their visit not be publicized, and Israel complied.

Main Archeological Findings:[23] Well-preserved remnants of the abovementioned Herodian road are much in evidence here. The road—Jerusalem's main thoroughfare at the end of the Second Temple period—is paved with large stone slabs and bordered by curbstones; beneath it are two drainage channels. On the paved road were found building stones of the walls of the Temple Mount that had accumulated there, and that soldiers of the Roman Legion had dismantled and rolled out of the compound after the Temple was burned and the mount conquered. These heavy stones smashed into the paving stones, causing them to sink and even penetrate the drainage channel beneath them.

Near the southwestern corner of the Temple Mount were found parts of the Robinson Arch, which the American biblical scholar Edward Robinson first identified in 1838. The

arch was built above the paved road as part of an overpass that enabled pedestrians to climb onto the mount from the Herodian road below. Adjacent to it were built smaller and smaller arches southward in a row. This series of arches supported a staircase on which people ascended from the road onto the mount. One of the stones of the Western Wall, under Robinson's Arch, bears the Hebrew inscription: "When you see this your heart shall rejoice, and their bones shall flourish like grass" (quoted with a slight change from Isaiah 66:14). To this inscription (whose time is not known, though it is generally dated from the Byzantine era onward) the excavators gave differing explanations.

9.3 The Western Wall Tunnel: The Excavation of the Underground Layers along the Full Length of the Western Wall (1968-1985)

Background: In 1968, the State of Israel, via its Religious Affairs Ministry, began to excavate the full length of the Western Wall. In an initial stage the prayer plaza was widened, and deepened a layer and a half beneath the previous level. This led to the discovery, to the north of the plaza at that time, of Wilson's Arch, which was investigated by the British engineer Charles Wilson back in 1867. Earth and debris were cleared from the arch, and the excavators began to dig northward toward the obscured parts of the Western Wall. In this endeavor, which ended in 1985, two to three layers of the Western

Workers of the Israel Religious Affairs Ministry at the start of the project to uncover the entire underground length of the Western Wall, early 1970s. The claim that Israel seeks to topple the Western Wall is absurd; Israel has acted to preserve and strengthen the wall. (courtesy of the Western Wall Heritage Foundation)

Wall were excavated along its whole length. (In some places it was also uncovered to a height of six or seven layers.)[24]

The Muslims' Charges: The excavation undermines the foundations of the Temple Mount mosques and is aimed at toppling them. The excavation also damages the stability of the structures situated above them in the Muslim Quarter of the Old City.

The Answer to the Charges: Here, too, it should be noted that Israel has no interest in harming the Western Wall, the most precious site to Jews among all the walls of the Temple Mount. Here, too, the charges were investigated several times by experts from the Technion and UNESCO and by engineers from the Religious Affairs Ministry, and it was found that the work had no effect on the stability of the Western Wall. Nevertheless, in several cases a link was found between the stability of structures in the Muslim Quarter and the digs carried out beneath it. Israel took each of these cases seriously and dealt with them immediately.[25]

Cautionary and Safety Measures Taken by Israel: Unlike the digs at the foot of the Southern Wall and the southern part of the Western Wall, which were carried out by the Antiquities Authority, the excavation of the Western Wall Tunnel was performed over the years by the Religious Affairs Ministry, under supervision of the Antiquities Authority and with engineering supervision by the ministry itself. Initially the engineer Meir Kuznits supervised the work, subsequently the engineer Naftali Kidron. Throughout, the ministry's engineering supervision was assisted by external experts, particularly from the Technion. In the 1970s, 1980s, and 1990s, the ministry's experts also took into account the professional assessments of UNESCO emissary Prof. Raymond Lamar, who submitted reports to his organization about the nature, process, and safety of the digs; some of his recommendations were implemented.

The tunnels' walls were buttressed with thick concrete girders, which were reinforced with iron beams. At the ground level above the tunnel, there are building foundations from various periods. This ground level consists of a mix of earth and ancient building remnants. For the most part the ground above the excavation site is saturated with organic material that came from cesspools—the bathrooms of those days. The shear strength of the ground in this area changed with every change in the degree of dampness.

When in the past the cesspools were flooded, or too much rainwater was absorbed into the ground, the stability of some of the buildings in the vicinity was weakened. The excavations in the Western Wall Tunnel were carried out only a few meters under these buildings. Hence the engineers of the Religious Affairs Ministry and of the Supervisory Department of the City of Jerusalem carried out regular surveillance checks of the buildings' stability, and when it was necessary to stop the work so as to strengthen them, that is what was done. Sometimes engineers of the Wakf, which is officially subordinate to the Jordanian government, were also allowed to take part and the Israeli engineers' maps were spread before them. In 1984, for example, excavation work in the tunnel was halted to allow the reinforcement of the foundations of the Majlis building, a fourteenth-century Mamluk structure where the Wakf has its offices. Under the ground thick iron nets were spread, and concrete walls were poured onto these. In other cases, building foundations in the area were reinforced with special adhesives or concrete anchors.[26]

Today, when the excavation work of the Western Wall has concluded, once a month a safety committee meets whose members are representatives of the Western Wall Heritage Foundation, the two external engineers, Antiquities Authority representatives, and a safety adviser. A comprehensive engineering survey was also done; it mapped all the recesses that were excavated and cleaned along the Western Wall Tunnel. In this context problems were dealt with in various ways including bluing, metal anchors, and the injection of lime-based binding material. The engineering survey also mapped all the stones of the Western Wall. The date of each stone's mapping, its condition, and recommendations on how to treat it were all recorded.

In many cases the reinforcement of the ancient recesses excavated along the Western Wall Tunnel rescued the houses above from sinking and collapse due to natural wear and tear.

In many cases it was the reinforcement of the ancient recesses excavated along the Western Wall Tunnel that rescued the houses above from sinking and collapse due to natural wear and tear. As noted, some of the houses are built on cesspools, which drain garbage and human waste into the ancient recesses and rooms along the tunnel. These recesses were cleaned, treated, and preserved. Some of the owners of these houses rejected a proposal from the Western Wall Heritage Foundation to deal with the sewage and sanitation system, or made this conditional on an overall renovation of their homes. In some cases the foundation fulfilled the demand (which included an element of extortion) and devoted large sums to a comprehensive renovation of homes above the tunnel, solely to prevent damage to the houses' stability, or their collapse and the resultant damage to the findings in the tunnel.[27] It should be noted that Israel did not oppose international supervision and involvement in ensuring the safety and reinforcement of dilapidated buildings above the tunnel. For example, the Egyptian consul and the Turkish ambassador were given tours, and the possibility was raised that they would assist with the matter.[28]

A typical recess of the Western Wall Tunnel before engineering and safety modifications. On the ceiling of the vault is an opening that drains sewage and garbage from the building above. (courtesy of the Western Wall Heritage Foundation)

Informal Muslim Attitudes: The main fear of the Wakf and the Supreme Muslim Council was that these excavations and the findings resulting from them might strengthen the Jewish claim to the Temple Mount and weaken the Muslim connection to it. They also frequently charged that the digs were aimed at toppling the mosques. Many of the Israelis involved got the impression that their concern about the stability of the

Muslim Quarter buildings was genuine. At the start of the 1970s, the heads of the Wakf and the Supreme Muslim Council unofficially visited the tunnels many times. One of the visits early in that decade also included the Muslim historian Arf al-Arf. He requested that the Israeli side define the nature of the excavation, religious or archeological, and remarked (apparently out of ignorance) that Prof. Mazar's digs to the south of the mount had not turned up any Jewish findings, only Muslim ones. Some of the participants in this tour asked for confirmation that Israel had no intention to deviate eastward from the north-south route, along which the Western Wall was being excavated for hundreds of meters.[29] In recent years the heads of the Wakf and the Muslim Council were also invited to visit the tunnels, but they repeatedly declined. The rabbi of the Western Wall, Rabbi Shmuel Rabinovich, recalls that during his tenure (since 1995) the Muslim leaders only once accepted an invitation to visit the tunnels and other sites that were under the aegis of the Western Wall Heritage Foundation.[30]

Main Archeological Findings:[31] About 350 meters of the underground layers of the Western Wall were excavated over the years, north of the open prayer plaza. By 1985, when this work ended, the picture was complete: the Western Wall extends for a good distance. The excavators not only revealed layers of the western retaining wall of the Temple Mount compound that once rose to about the same height as the wall does today above the open prayer plaza; they also excavated what was called the "secret passage," built in the Middle Ages and mentioned in fifteenth-century Mamluk sources. This passage became an entrance to the site of the tunnels. Also excavated was a system of vaults from the Roman period and the Muslim period that extends from the "secret passage" and creates a bridge over the Tyropoeon Valley, which separates between the Temple Mount and the hill where the Jewish and Armenian quarters stand. The bridge leads away from the remnant of a giant stone junction of Second Temple days that is called Wilson's Arch.

The access tunnel to the Western Wall Tunnel, which was uncovered for the entire length of its 488 meters. (courtesy of the Western Wall Heritage Foundation)

At the lower level at the end of the "secret passage," the Herodian Hall was excavated. There catapult stones were found, a sort of mute testimony to the great battle against the Romans. Northward from there was discovered, cleaned, and renovated the largest of the rooms of the Western Wall Tunnel, apparently from the Ayyubid era; in it was placed a model of the Temple Mount and the Temple in the Second Temple period. The excavation of the full length of the Western Wall again revealed the wonders of Herodian-era construction.

In his book on the Western Wall tunnels, the archeologist Dr. Dan Bahat[32] explains that the layers of the Western Wall "were not placed one on top of the other, identically and precisely in a perpendicular line, but by a special method in which each layer was moved inward by about two centimeters from the layer beneath it. This way of laying the stones was aimed at giving an impressive appearance of abundance and stability." The Herodian layers of the visible Western Wall are one to one and one-fourth meters high; but much more imposing Herodian stones were found along the walls of the tunnels. The largest of these is 13.60 meters long with an estimated depth of 3.5-4.6 meters and a height of 3.3 meters; its weight comes to about six hundred tons. The quarry from which this stone was taken, and other stones of similar dimensions, apparently was located north of the Temple Mount in the area that is higher than the mount, so that the stones did not have to be lifted but instead could be lowered to the right level at a moderate incline.

The stone with the huge dimensions is adjacent to Warren's Gate, one of the four gates to the Temple Mount at the Western Wall in the late Second Temple period. A bit north of Warren's Gate is the spot known as "Facing the Holy of Holies." This is believed to be the closest point to the Temple's Holy of Holies, which was located on the mount about two thousand years ago. Walking north, one comes to a Mamluk cistern and two shafts that descend beneath the modern walking level to the Second Temple-era street level. Toward the end of the narrow tunnel is another cistern (from the Hasmonean period), an open stretch of road from Second Temple days, and segments where the Western Wall stones were, unlike the other segments, chiseled in natural rock.

One should also mention the unearthing of the foundation layers of the Western Wall in the summer of 2011, at their lowest point near the southern end of the wall. These layers were submerged underground even in the Second Temple era. The archeologists Prof. Ronny Reich and Eli Shukron, who uncovered them along a length of eleven meters, note that even the pilgrims of the Second Temple period could not see them. These foundation stones are less smooth than the stones of the Western Wall that rise above the open plaza, and it is evident that Herod's builders shaped them relatively crudely since they served as foundations and were sunken in the earth.[33]

9.4 The Uncovering of the Hasmonean Channel and the Opening of the Exit Gate to the Via Dolorosa (1987-1996)

Background: The Hasmonean (water) Channel was connected to the Western Wall Tunnel and newly uncovered both to reinvestigate it and, primarily, to use it as an exit route for a tour that begins at Wilson's Arch, beside the Western Wall prayer plaza, and ends at the Via Dolorosa. The aim was to lead the numerous visitors and tourists through this unique underground site.

The continuation of the Western Wall Tunnel: the Hasmonean Channel. Despite the Palestinians' claim, the channel does not pass under the Temple Mount compound at all. It existed for about nine hundred years before the mosques on the mount were built, having been dug as a waterworks in the Hasmonean era. Israel merely uncovered it anew. (courtesy of the Western Wall Heritage Foundation)

Before an exit gate from the Hasmonean Channel was opened, the end point and exit point for the thousands of visitors were the same: the Western Wall plaza. People entered the tunnel, came to its end, and retraced their steps within its narrow space, returning to the plaza. This greatly curtailed the number of visitors to the site. Once a gate was opened at the end of the Hasmonean Channel, visitors could conclude their tour aboveground in the Old City's markets, and other groups could enter the tunnel without waiting for the previous groups to exit. Hence the number of visitors to the Western Wall Tunnel and the Hasmonean Channel greatly increased. Each year eight hundred thousand people, including both Israeli visitors and foreign tourists, come to these sites.[34]

The Muslims' Charges: In September 1996, a few hours after Israel opened the exit gate from the Hasmonean Channel to the Via Dolorosa for the public, thousands of incensed Muslims—led by Palestinian policemen—attacked IDF forces and Israeli citizens in most areas of the West Bank. In what came to be called the Western Wall Tunnel

Yasser Arafat denied the existence of a Jewish Temple on the Temple Mount and accused the Israeli government of instigating attacks on the mosques there. (AP Photo)

riots, fifteen IDF soldiers were killed and about seventy Israeli civilians and soldiers injured. On the Palestinian side there were forty fatalities and over six hundred injured. The riots came hand in hand with fierce proclamations by the Palestinian leadership. Palestinian Authority chairman Yasser Arafat called the opening of the gate "a crime against our religion that flouts the peace process and the Oslo accords."[35] The Arab League declared that "Israel's aim in opening this gate is to cause the collapse of the Al-Aksa Mosque, so that it can build the Third Temple in its stead."[36] Spokesmen for the Palestinian Authority, the Jordanian government, as well as the Wakf chief in East Jerusalem, Abd al-Azim Salhub, made similar statements. As the rhetoric got more and more virulent, the terminology changed as well. The Hasmonean Channel came to be called the Al-Aksa Tunnel, and the Palestinian demonstrators were dubbed "warriors of Al-Aksa."[37]

The Answer to the Charges: The Western Wall Tunnel and the Hasmonean Channel run northward from the open prayer plaza to the foot of the Western Wall. The Western Wall Tunnel, which reopened the lower layers of the Western Wall along a length of 350 meters, was an excavation of preexisting underground recesses. Its continuation, the Hasmonean Channel, which was linked to the tunnel and which also runs north-south, was not excavated in our time but, rather, newly uncovered. Originally this channel was hewn out of rock more than two thousand years ago. A researcher, Charles Warren, already floated on its waters in the nineteenth century.[38] All that Israeli archeologists, as well as personnel of the Religious Affairs Ministry, did was to clear the channel of mud and long-accumulated cesspool waters, reinforce it with iron and cement, and make this spectacular archeological site available to the public.

Like the Western Wall Tunnel, the Hasmonean Channel runs along a north-south axis; but unlike the tunnel, of which it is a continuation, it extends further northward, for another 80 meters, toward the northwestern end of the Temple Mount wall, under the Convent of the Sisters of Zion on the Via Dolorosa. The charge that the excavation of the channel endangers the mosques is simply a tall tale. The dig does not pass under the Temple Mount compound at all, and the channel existed about nine hundred years before the Temple Mount mosques were built, when it was dug as a waterworks in the Hasmonean era (from the second to the first century BCE)—or in some researchers' view even earlier. The allegation that the excavation desecrates a Muslim holy place is likewise baseless, since even according to the maximalist approach, which regards the entire Temple Mount compound and its walls as a Muslim holy place, the Hasmonean Channel does not intersect with the walls or the mount but runs separately and northward from them. In any case, it is a fact that the Hasmonean Channel existed long before the Al-Aksa Mosque. Even after the mosque was built, the channel never undermined, let alone destroyed it, any more than the Western Wall Tunnel ever has.

Note also that the Muslims discussed (albeit informally) with the Israeli authorities a "deal" whereby Solomon's Stables would be used as a mosque in return for the opening and quiet use of the Hasmonean Channel along with an exit from it. The fact that such a deal was mutually explored, and the readiness in principle to consider the opening and use of the Hasmonean Channel, reveals that the Muslims did not really believe the channel constituted a danger to the mosques. If they had, they would never have negotiated about opening it.

The fact that the Muslims discussed a deal to enable the opening of the Hasmonean Channel in return for converting Solomon's Stables into a mosque reveals that they did not really believe the channel constituted a danger to the Al-Aksa Mosque.

Cautionary and Safety Measures Taken by Israel: Here, too, periodic safety inspections are carried out. The reinforcements are minimal because the Hasmonean Channel is a superb aqueduct hewn from rock that sustained itself, until being uncovered anew, for over two thousand years without incurring any sort of damage. Most of the alteration of the tunnel route was done so that visitors could walk through it safely and included railings, lighting, and other safety accessories.

Informal Muslim Attitudes: Such attitudes have not been documented, but at the end of June 1997 the Arab League decided to designate an annual day in September (the 25th) for identification with Jerusalem. On this day schools were to teach the Muslim history of Jerusalem and ways to counter efforts to Judaize the city.[39]

Main Archeological Findings:[40] The Hasmonean Channel is about 80 meters long. Its average height is 7 meters (12 at the highest point) and its width is 1.2 meters. The channel was dug as an open canal from the ground surface downward; subsequently it was covered with heavy stone slabs that are still visible. The aqueduct segment on which visitors walk today is the southern segment of the original aqueduct, which led out from the northern part of the city, next to the Damascus Gate. There, apparently, the cesspool waters of the Tyropoeon stream were drained toward a Hasmonean fortress that was called *birah* and stood beside the Hasmonean Temple Mount. Later, evidently in Herod's time, a large pool was installed at the northern end of the aqueduct to hoard its waters. For unclear reasons, in Second Temple days this pool was given the name Struthion, which means "lark" in Greek. Most of the pool is under the Convent of the Sisters of Zion on the Via Dolorosa. In the late 1860s, the British researcher Charles Warren visited the pool and, on an improvised raft, floated a few dozen meters into the southern part of the aqueduct south of the pool. His voyage alarmed the Sisters of Zion, who feared that unknown persons would try to infiltrate the convent via the part of the pool that was in their territory; hence they built a wall that divided the pool in two. The north-south walking route within the channel is at a moderate upward incline.

9.5 The Excavation and Preparation of the Passages Under the Ohel Yitzchak Synagogue on Haggai Street (2004-2008)

Background:[41] The Ohel Yitzchak Synagogue stands some 60 meters west of the Western Wall. The site served as a synagogue owned by the Shomrei Hachomot (Guardians of the Walls) *kollel* (institute for fulltime advanced Jewish study) from the time it was built in 1917 (on a plot of land the *kollel* purchased from the Khaladi family in 1867) until it was abandoned during the 1936 riots. Up to the 1930s, in this vicinity and other parts of what is now called the Muslim Quarter, thousands of Jews lived and maintained numerous Torah and charity institutions. The synagogue stood intact for only thirty-one years, and then in 1948 was blown up by the Jordanians along with other Old City synagogues. Complete sections of the building, however, survived. In 1993, the ruined structure was purchased by the family of American Jewish philanthropist Irving Moskowitz. In 2004, the Antiquities Authority began to dig beneath the synagogue's remains and unearthed priceless findings mainly from the late Muslim period. The synagogue itself was reconstructed with the help of old photographs and rebuilt with the cooperation and supervision of the Antiquities Authority.

The Ohel Yitzchak Synagogue before the Arabs destroyed it, early twentieth century. (courtesy of the Western Wall Heritage Foundation)

The Ohel Yitzchak Synagogue after the Arabs destroyed it; the Dome of the Rock is in the background. (Western Wall Heritage Foundation)

The Ohel Yitzchak Synagogue after its renovation and reconstruction (Nadav Shragai). The synagogue overlooks the Temple Mount from the west. The work of renovating has no connection to the mount, which is tens of meters distant from it.

The Muslims' Charges: "Israel is digging clandestinely under the Al-Aksa Mosque on the Temple Mount, with the aim of erecting the Third Temple....These excavations mark a very dangerous phase in the history of the mosque" (Sheikh Raed Salah, January 21, 2007).[42] For years Muslim circles have been disseminating pictures through the media of the excavations being done under the Ohel Yitzchak Synagogue. They claim this is proof that Israel is digging under the Temple Mount compound.

The Answer to the Charges: The Ohel Yitzchak Synagogue stands at the southern end of Haggai Street, not far from the covered passage through which tourists and visitors enter the open prayer plaza of the Western Wall. As mentioned, the synagogue that has been reconstructed and rebuilt by the Antiquities Authority and the Western Wall Heritage Foundation is about 60 meters west of the Western Wall. The excavation beneath it not only is not being conducted under the Temple Mount but does not even extend as far as the Western Wall itself. The secondary "excavation," which actually is not an excavation but an unearthing and cleaning operation under existing vaults, was initiated to link the area of the excavations under Ohel Yitzchak to the entry rooms to the Western Wall Tunnel, which stand a few dozen meters to the west of the Western Wall.

Hence this excavation, too, is not being done under the mount and does not even reach the wall. An educational center on the subject of prayer is being planned at Ohel Yitzchak, along with a museum for bar mitzvah youth. The purpose of the underground link between the two facilities is to enable some visitors to the Western Wall Tunnel, mainly children, to end the tour in the area adjacent to the wall and not, like most visitors, on the Via Dolorosa. The excavations at the place are not being done surreptitiously as the Muslims claim. They have been displayed more than once to the media, and publications about them have appeared on the Antiquities Authority's website and at professional conferences that are open to the general public.

Here, too, as with the Western Wall Tunnel, the excavation actually salvaged the houses located above the distorted vaults, which were in danger of collapse due to their age and condition.

Cautionary and Safety Measures Taken by Israel:[43] In the underground recesses revealed during the excavation and cleaning operations under Ohel Yitzchak, it also was found that some of the vaults suffered from major distortions and some of their weight-bearing capacity had been severely damaged. Here, too, as with several of the rooms of the Western Wall Tunnel, the excavation actually salvaged the houses located above the distorted vaults, which were in danger of collapse due to their age and condition. Because of the uncertain stability of the vaults, it was decided not to carry out any operations on them until they had been fully supported with steel bracing designed for heavy loads. This bracing was planned to withstand loads of up to ten tons per meter. Once the bracing of the vaults was finished, preservation operations were performed that also included dismantlement and rebuilding or recasting of some of the most distorted vaults. The bracing was done by strengthening the steel with reinforced concrete in the entire area of the vaults that required support, as well as a set of steel pillars with steel webbing above them. Within the steel webbing a steel mesh was emplaced so as to reduce to a minimum the possibility of the sliding of some of the vaults. Above the steel webbing was added a contact level made of a rigid cement substance, thereby creating a continuity of support for the vaults.

The underground recesses under the destroyed Ohel Yitzchak Synagogue, which the Jordanians blew up and the Israelis rehabilitated. These recesses are connected to the Western Wall Tunnel compound, but despite Muslim claims they do not reach the Temple Mount and indeed are tens of meters distant from it. (courtesy of the Western Wall Heritage Foundation)

Informal Muslim Attitudes: None have been documented.

Main Archeological Findings:[44] Under the remains of the Ohel Yitzchak Synagogue the archeologists Dr. Chaim Baraba, Tawfik Da'adla, and Dr. Avi Solomon discovered a large bathhouse from the Mamluk period (apparently from the fourteenth century CE). The dressing room was fully preserved, and remnants were found of the heating stoves that radiated steam, as well as a dual system of flow channels that brought warm air into the bathhouse chambers. In the opinion of Jerusalem district archeologist Dr. Yuval Baruch, this is the most complete Mamluk structure to have been excavated in Jerusalem. Also discovered at the site were remains of walls and a staircase from the ancient Roman period; walls from the late Roman period; parts of the secondary cardo[45] from that period, with paving stones of impressive size (1.6 meters long and 1 meter wide); plaster flooring and potsherds from the ancient Muslim period; and building remnants from the Crusader-Ayyubid period.

9.6 The Inauguration of the Hurva Synagogue (March 15, 2010)

Background:[46] The rebuilt Hurva Synagogue (its original official name is Beit Yaakov), in the heart of the Jewish Quarter of the Old City of Jerusalem, was inaugurated in a state ceremony on March 15, 2010. In the first half of the twentieth century the Hurva Synagogue became a symbol and a center for religious and national events for the Jews of Jerusalem. The synagogue was very splendid, widely renowned, and from a scenic standpoint it became part of the Jerusalem skyline along with the Christian Church of the Holy Sepulchre and the Muslim Dome of the Rock.

In 1700, the Ashkenazi community of Jerusalem built a synagogue in the area where eventually the Hurva Synagogue would stand. This house of prayer was erected on the eve of the arrival in Jerusalem from Poland of Rabbi Yehuda Hasid and a group of his students. Twenty years later a Muslim mob destroyed the synagogue and the surrounding houses ("Court of the Ashkenazim") because of the nonpayment of debts for loans that were taken by Rabbi Yehuda Hasid's students. The site remained in ruins until the mid-nineteenth century, coming to be known as the "Court of Destruction" (hurva). In 1836, the Ottomans gave Rabbi Avraham Shlomo Zalman Tsoref a firman to build a small synagogue at the site (the Menachem Tsion Synagogue), and in 1855 the Ottomans also gave the philanthropist Moses Montefiore a firman to build another synagogue there, larger and more imposing; this is the Beit Yaakov Synagogue, also known as Hurva. It was inaugurated in 1864 and gradually became a center for Jewish life, both in old and renewed Jerusalem. In Hurva the Ashkenazi chief rabbis of Jerusalem and the Land of Israel were appointed. From Hurva a call to rescue the Jews of Europe was issued by a prayer-and-fasting assembly of hundreds of rabbis; at Hurva prayers were held for the coronation of George V as king of England; and there, too, Zeev Jabotinsky staged a recruitment rally for the Jewish Legion. Even Herzl visited the place in 1898, viewing the city from the balcony that surrounded the dome of the building. Shortly before the Jewish Quarter fell and its defenders were captured by Jordan in May 1948, the Jordanian Legion blew up the synagogue along with other synagogues and Torah institutions in the Old City.

Shortly before the Jewish Quarter fell and its defenders were captured by Jordan in May 1948, the Jordanian Legion blew up the Hurva Synagogue along with other synagogues and Torah institutions in the Old City.

The commander of the Jordanian Legion battalion that conquered the quarter, Abdullah al-Tal, put it in these terms: "For the first time in a thousand years, not a single Jew remained in the Jewish Quarter and not a single building remained there that was not damaged. This makes the return of the Jews impossible."[47] Yet in 1967 the Jews returned, and in 2004 the Israeli government began to raise up Hurva from the ruins. By 2010 that task was completed.

The Muslims' Charges: The mufti of the Palestinian territories, Sheikh Muhammad Hussein, charged that the Jews had rebuilt the Hurva Synagogue as preparation for the building of the Temple.[48] Sheikh Raed Salah spoke of an Israeli attempt to encircle the Al-Aksa Mosque with synagogues.[49] The supreme *sharia* judge of the Palestinian Authority, Taysir al-Tamimi, said that "in keeping with the Israeli and Jewish plans, which have been approved by the Israeli government, from the Hurva Synagogue Israel can storm the Al-Aksa Mosque and destroy it."[50] Even Palestinian Authority chairman Mahmoud Abbas said regarding the synagogue's inauguration that "saving Jerusalem is a personal duty for all of us and we are determined to protect the capital of Palestine."[51]

For two days after the inauguration, riots erupted in many parts of the West Bank and with particular intensity in Jerusalem. Again it was charged that Israel was aiming to harm the Al-Aksa Mosque and build the Third Temple in its place. Khaled Mashaal, chairman of Hamas' political bureau, declared that "the inauguration of the Hurva Synagogue spells the destruction of the Al-Aksa Mosque and the building of the Temple."[52] Khatam Abd al-Kadr, who holds the Jerusalem portfolio in the Fatah movement, claimed in an interview with Palestinian radio that the presence at the inauguration of members of Israel's governing coalition attested that "this is a first step toward the building of the Third Temple on the ruins of the Al-Aksa Mosque."[53] On the day after the inauguration, a rumor circulated in eastern Jerusalem that Israel had dug a tunnel linking the basement of the Hurva Synagogue to the Temple Mount compound.[54]

The Answer to the Charges: Given the Hurva Synagogue's location and its height relative to the Temple Mount, it is not even theoretically possible that its construction could undermine the stability of the mosques. The synagogue's foundations were dug at a point dozens of meters higher than the mount compound. As for the rumor of a tunnel leading from the synagogue to the mount, it was a product of fantasy. The Hurva Synagogue is situated in the Jewish Quarter about 400 meters southwest of the mount, and its ground level is about 50 meters higher than that of the mosques.

Concealed by the "Al-Aksa is in danger" incitement campaign is the fact that the Hurva Synagogue far exceeds the height of the Al-Aksa Mosque and the Dome of the Rock. In 1855, with the granting of the *firman* to build Hurva, the Jews decided to erect a large, magnificent synagogue in the Hurva courtyard that would be comparable to other beautiful religious edifices in Jerusalem. A researcher of Hurva and the period, Arie Morgenstern, recently discovered[55] that the Ottoman architect Assad Effendi happened to be in Jerusalem that same year, having been sent from Istanbul by the sultan to supervise a repair of the Temple Mount mosques. Assad Effendi agreed to the Jews' request that he plan and supervise the synagogue's construction. It appears that it was the involvement of the sultan's architect himself that led to the plan's approval. Previously, the Muslim authorities had not allowed the building of prominent religious structures that would exceed their own structures in height and stature.

The magnificent Hurva Synagogue, approved in 1855, was planned and supervised by the Ottoman sultan's architect Assad Effendi.

The great height of the Hurva Synagogue—24 meters from floor to dome—was mortifying to its Muslim neighbors and the Muslim clergy. With the Jewish Quarter's fall to Jordanian forces in the War of Independence, the Jordanian Legion could have used the Hurva Synagogue along with its neighbor, the Tiferet Yisrael Synagogue (also known as Nissan Beck), as command posts; instead it hastened to blow them up and erase what had been an impressive Jewish presence facing the Temple Mount.[56] When Hurva was rebuilt by the Israeli government, and indeed reconstructed in its original form, its great height and splendor once again was a bitter pill for the Muslims. That is the real reason for their wrath over its reconstruction and inauguration. Clear indications of this could be found in the Palestinian media and various statements by Palestinian leaders. For example, on March 16, 2010, the Ramallah newspaper *Al-Ayyam* published a cartoon in which the synagogue appears as a high, huge mushroom that overshadows the Dome of the Rock and the Al-Aksa Mosque, which appear beside it as two particularly low structures.[57] That same day Palestinian television broadcast the anti-Israeli documentary *Synagogues Surround Al-Aksa*, while Azzat al-Shark, a member of the Hamas political bureau, said that "the building of the Hurva Synagogue is tantamount to a declaration of war, since it constitutes a direct threat to the Al-Aksa Mosque."[58] Other Muslim spokesmen made statements in the same spirit.

Informal Muslim Attitudes: None have been documented.

Main Archeological Findings: As noted, there is no connection between the rebuilding of the Hurva Synagogue and the stability of the Temple Mount mosques, just as there is none between the rescue dig, which was mandated by Israeli law before construction could begin in a historical vicinity, and the Temple Mount compound. The rescue dig under the Hurva Synagogue uncovered sections of walls and fragments of pottery from the First Temple period. From the late Second Temple or Herodian era, remnants of a residence including rooms and *mikvehs* were found; from the Byzantine era, the stone pavement of a narrow street with an entirely preserved arch above it was uncovered. Building remains dating from the ancient Muslim period to the Ottoman era were unearthed as well. A surprise awaited the excavators when they came upon a forgotten weapons cache including grenades and mortar bombs—left there by the Irgun underground while they were fighting to eject British rule from the Land of Israel in pre-statehood days.

9.7 The Excavations at the Mughrabi Gate Access Ramp (2007)

Background: The Mughrabi Gate access ramp was an earthen ramp that led—until its partial collapse in 2004—to the Mughrabi Gate, which opens from the southern part of the Western Wall into the Temple Mount plaza. The gate and the ramp that led to it are known as the Mughrabi Quarter, in which about 650 people, mostly North African Muslims, lived until it was evacuated and leveled by Israel after the Six-Day War. This was done to prepare the prayer plaza at the foot of the Western Wall for hundreds of thousands of Jewish worshippers. The narrow Western Wall alley that the Mughrabi homes had bordered could accommodate no more than a few hundred worshippers.[59]

Since 1967, the Mughrabi Gate has been the only entrance gate to the Temple Mount compound through which non-Muslims can pass, including Israeli Jews and Jewish

The earthen ramp that served as a bridge to the Mughrabi Gate, after weather conditions caused its collapse in the winter of 2004. (courtesy of the Western Wall Heritage Foundation)

The temporary wooden bridge that Israel built to replace the collapsed ramp. It is not used by Muslim worshippers, who have many other entrances to the Temple Mount. The Mughrabi Gate is the sole entrance to the Temple Mount for Jews, tourists, and Israeli security forces since the Six-Day War. (Western Wall Heritage Foundation)

tourists, Christians, and others. The gate also serves the security forces in times of crisis. And the Mughrabi Gate is the only entrance to the compound whose keys are in the hands of the Israel Police.[60]

On February 14, 2004, as a result of an earthquake and snowfall that damaged the stability of the ramp, a segment of its northern retaining wall collapsed, as well as its northern section.[61] The landslide had to be fenced off and dealt with immediately. In a short time a temporary wooden bridge was planned and built so that people could keep entering the Temple Mount through the Mughrabi Gate. At the same time, planning began for a permanent solution to enable access to the mount in place of the collapsed structure.

In November 2006, the Local Planning Committee of the City of Jerusalem approved the construction of a permanent bridge, then issued a building permit, subject to a few conditions. These measures sparked protests over the planning, political, and archeological aspects. The Ir Amim movement[62] claimed, for example, that a detailed city building plan was required, which should be made available for public objections before the building permit was issued. The government's legal adviser affirmed that a city building plan should be prepared for the new access ramp in a transparent planning procedure.

In light of this assessment, then-Jerusalem Mayor Uri Lupolianski canceled the building permit. In October 2007, the District Planning and Building Committee

The archeological rescue digs of the Israel Antiquities Authority, which enabled the building of the Mughrabi Bridge to replace the collapsed ramp. Israel allowed UNESCO, Turkey, and anyone else who so desired to visit the place. (courtesy of the Israel Antiquities Authority)

decided to open the updated report for public objections, and in May 2008 it was approved with a number of restrictions. The National Planning and Building Council approved and authorized the plan as well.[63] Given its political sensitivity, however, (as of January 2012) Prime Minister Benjamin Netanyahu delayed its implementation[64] even though a building permit had already been issued.[65]

Hand in hand with the planning procedure, whose aim was to create a permanent replacement for the collapsed ramp, in February 2007 the Antiquities Authority began an archeological dig in the vicinity of the collapsed ramp in light of the various construction options being considered for the alternative bridge. The Antiquities Authority set several conditions for the alternative bridge, which was planned to extend from the area of the Archeological Garden at the southwestern corner of the Temple Mount to the Mughrabi Gate: (1) that the bridge would not obstruct the mount, (2) that rescue digs would be conducted at the site as mandated by the law, before the bridge was built, and (3) that the location of the columns supporting the bridge would be decided only after the digs, since no one could know what antiquities would be discovered there.

Among the Palestinians, the Islamic Movement in Israel, and particularly Hamas, the Antiquities Authority's activity at the Mughrabi Gate access ramp triggered a systematic campaign that portrayed the work as an Israeli attempt to destroy the Al-Aksa Mosque.

Among the Palestinians, the Islamic Movement in Israel, and particularly Hamas, the Antiquities Authority's activity at the site triggered a systematic campaign that portrayed the work being conducted at the Mughrabi Gate, and the different plans pertaining to it, as an Israeli attempt to destroy the Al-Aksa Mosque.

The Muslims' Charges: On February 4, 2007, head of the Hamas political bureau Khaled Mashaal held a press conference in Damascus that addressed, among other things, "the attack Israel is mounting on the Al-Aksa Mosque."[66] Mashaal charged that the "Israeli enemy" was planning a further crime against the mosque, namely, the destruction of the Mughrabi Gate access ramp, which was a "historical pathway to the Al-Aksa Mosque." He called on the Palestinians to awaken and focus their struggle on Israel. Hamas prime minister Ismail Haniyeh accused the "Israeli occupation" of continuing its aggression against the Al-Aksa Mosque.[67] Hamas' satellite TV channel devoted most of its broadcasts at this time to short incendiary clips about what it called "the danger hovering over Jerusalem." The channel featured pictures of the renovation and excavation work at the site and drummed home the message of "the Israeli plot against the Al-Aksa Mosque."[68]

Palestinian Authority president Mahmoud Abbas was not to be outdone by Hamas. He proclaimed that "what Israel is doing at the Mughrabi Gate demonstrates its intentions and its deeds, planned in advance and entailing the destruction of the Muslim holy places."[69] PA television also joined the party and repeatedly broadcast talk shows and songs about the "danger to Al-Aksa." On February 4, it charged that Israeli settlers and "Zionist militias" had begun digging under the mosque and were threatening to destroy it.[70] Rafik al-Husseini, director of Abbas' bureau, visited Al-Aksa along with the heads of the Wakf and promised to provide all necessary assistance to the struggle against what he called the Jewish excavations under the Temple Mount.[71] Similar declarations were voiced in Damascus, where it was claimed that Israel had already demolished parts of the mount. Syrian cartoons in *Tishrin* in mid-February showed a stereotypical Jew digging beside Al-Aksa, about to release the safety catch of a grenade that would blow up the Middle East.[72]

Sheikh Raed Salah crossed all the lines with a sermon in Jerusalem's Wadi Joz neighborhood where he intoned that "Israeli history is filthy with blood. They want to build their Temple when our blood is on their clothes, on their doors, and in their food and drink. Our blood passes from one general to another terrorist general." Hundreds of Israeli Arabs came to the area of the Dung Gate, about a hundred meters from the Mughrabi Gate, to demonstrate against the Israeli project. Attorney Zahi Nujidat, spokesman of the northern branch of the Islamic Movement, said: "We think the aim of these activities is to declare Al-Aksa a synagogue."[73] Muhammad Zeidan, former chairman of the Higher Monitoring Committee, added that the digs were endangering the mosque.[74] It was charged as well that the Al-Buraq Mosque near the gate stood to be harmed.

The Answer to the Charges: Until its partial collapse, the Mughrabi Gate access ramp separated the prayer plaza at the foot of the Western Wall to the north from the area of the archeological digs, at the foot of the wall, to the south. The site that is the target of Muslim criticism borders the women's section of the Western Wall to the north, the upper plaza of the wall to the west, the Archeological Park to the south, and the Temple Mount to the east.

The work on the section of the ramp that collapsed, the archeological digs at this spot, and the building plan for the Mughrabi Bridge that is to replace the temporary wooden bridge that replaced the collapsed ramp—all are in a vicinity very close to the Temple Mount, about 80 meters north of its southwestern corner and not far from the Western Wall. Yet *the work has not extended into the Temple Mount compound and is not planned to do so.*

Moreover, in the face of Muslim sensitivities and the wild incitement, which sought to link the activity at the site to a supposed plan to dig under the Temple Mount and thereby bring down the mosques, the Antiquities Authority and the Israeli planning institutions went so far as to bend the law. According to Israel's Antiquities Law, an item is defined as an antiquity if it was created before the year 1700. Yet, in line with the demands of UNESCO and Ir Amim, it was decided also to preserve items of more recent vintage at the digs, including relics of the Mughrabi Quarter at the end of the Ottoman period and the Jordanian period, from less than a century ago.

And in keeping with a governmental decree, the Israeli archeologists also deliberately avoided excavating the Berkeley Gate even though, in terms of archeological logic and scientific interest, it would have been very rewarding to do so. This gate,[75] dating from Second Temple days, lies under the Mughrabi Gate. At present, only a section of its huge lintel on its external side has been revealed. This section of the lintel is visible from the women's section of the Western Wall and from a room that is under the Mughrabi Gate. The gate was built in Herod's time during the expansions of the Temple, and some identify it with what the Mishnah calls the "Kipunus Gate."[76]

The Muslims, despite their protestations, were not materially harmed by the collapse of the Mughrabi Gate access ramp and the building of the wooden bridge that serves as its temporary replacement; since 1967 the Mughrabi Gate has been used solely by non-Muslims as an entrance to the Temple Mount. The Muslims use many other gates to the mount, such as the Shalshelet or Cotton Merchants' gates. Indeed, it was only Jewish worshippers at the Western Wall plaza who were inconvenienced, since the building of the wooden bridge reduced the area of the women's section by about 50 percent. This has caused serious crowding, especially during holidays.

Regarding the supposed harm to the Al-Buraq Mosque, this underground mosque is on the eastern side of the Western Wall behind the Berkeley Gate, which Israeli archeologists refrained from excavating. There is only access to the internal side of the gate and to the Al-Buraq Mosque from within the Temple Mount via a staircase to the north of the Mughrabi Gate. Despite Muslim claims, the mosque is not on the western side of the Western Wall under the ramp of the Mughrabi Gate.

It is true that in 2004, when the collapse of the Mughrabi Gate access ramp occurred, a small room was discovered that included an alcove covered by a dome, a sort of Muslim prayer niche (*mihrab*) facing south. In the view of Jerusalem district archeologist Dr. Yuval Baruch,[77] however, the *mihrab* indicates that a Mamluk or Ottoman prayer structure stood at the spot; it was destroyed many years ago and nothing remained of it but the *mihrab* itself.[78] At that time Prof. Dan Bahat gave a similar assessment to the Western Wall Heritage Foundation.[79]

At the end of February 2007, a delegation of UNESCO experts came to Israel for four days to inspect the excavations at the Mughrabi Gate access ramp. On March 12, the delegation published a report[80] that completely exonerated Israel of damaging or threatening the Al-Aksa Mosque. Among other things, the delegation wrote: "No work is being conducted inside the Haram es-Sharif, nor may the nature of the works underway be reported, at this stage, as constituting a threat to the stability of the Western Wall and the Al-Aqsa Mosque" (para. 17). "The work area," the delegation explained, "ends at approximately 10 metres distance from the Western Wall. It is conducted with light equipment, picks and shovels, and it is supervised and documented according to professional standards" (para. 18). "The *Jerusalem Municipality* is responsible for planning and construction in the Old City, as well as for the infrastructure and its maintenance" (para. 23) (emphasis in original). "It was clearly and repeatedly stated, both by the IAA and by the religious authorities consulted by the mission, that there are no plans to conduct any excavation under the Haram es-Sharif" (para. 30).[81]

Ten days later, on March 21, 2007, a delegation of experts from Turkey visited the site. They, too, were persuaded that there was no damage from the Mughrabi Gate access ramp excavations and no connection between them and the stability of the Temple Mount mosques. The delegation, however, refrained from publishing these conclusions so as to maintain Turkey's good relations with Arab states, and the group's leader ceased to address the issue.[82]

Cautionary and Safety Measures Taken by Israel: Immediately after the ramp collapsed, the area was fenced off and access to it by visitors and worshippers was denied. As we saw, the Israeli archeologists showed great deference to the Muslims' complaints, despite the incitement that accompanied them. In the excavations' first days, in an attempt to defuse the suspicions and agitation, the Antiquities Authority positioned cameras at the excavation site that continuously broadcast the activity there.[83] At a certain stage the work was stopped by a directive of the minister responsible for the Antiquities Authority at that time, Raleb Majadele. As noted, Prime Minister Netanyahu declined to approve the start of construction of the new bridge because of the evident sensitivity of the site, as well as a demand by Jordan, which was involved in the planning, to carry out the construction itself.[84] Cabinet ministers and senior officials on the operative governmental level believe the prime minister should give a green light to this project. The question of the safety of the temporary wooden bridge has also been raised publicly. Both the Western Wall Heritage Foundation and the Jerusalem municipality feared for its stability and demanded its quick replacement with a stable permanent bridge. In May 2011, Shlomo Eshkol, chief engineer of the City of Jerusalem, strongly urged the Western Wall Heritage Foundation to dismantle the temporary bridge due to its "faulty structural condition."[85]

Twice a date was announced for replacing the temporary bridge with a permanent one (June and November 2011), but the action was postponed each time out of concern that this would harm Israel's relations with Egypt and Jordan. Both nations were suffering the effects of instability in light of the revolution in Egypt and the political changes in neighboring Arab countries known as the "Arab Spring." Israel feared that the anger of the masses in both countries, who at that very time were demonstrating in the streets over other issues, would be directed at the Jewish state and would endanger the peace agreements with Jordan and Egypt. In the end, the Israeli government decided in December 2011 to renovate and strengthen the temporary bridge until a more suitable opportunity arose to replace it with a permanent bridge.

Informal Muslim Attitudes: None have been documented.

Main Archeological Findings:[86] The Mughrabi Gate access ramp excavations that began on February 11, 2007, revealed remnants of houses from the Mughrabi Quarter that were there until 1967. By July the remains of about twenty rooms were unearthed. Ceramics as well as coins from the Ottoman period, which date the time of the building of the rooms, were discovered under their floors. On the floors themselves were many items from the twentieth century including bronze basins, cooking and table utensils, glass bottles, shoes, and so on. Numerous coins, mostly Jordanian dinars, were also found.

At the northern part of the ramp, the excavation reached the level of the Western Wall plaza. An area was dug there beneath a layer from the Ottoman period, where the walls of the houses from this era were built upon walls from the Mamluk period and on even older walls, from the twelfth to thirteenth centuries CE. These remnants led archeologists to hypothesize that there had been continuous settlement since the neighborhood's founding. As noted, the remains of a *mihrab* of a prayer building, destroyed at an unknown time, were also found buried there.

9.8 The Archeological Digs at the City of David Since 1967

Background: Immediately after wresting Jerusalem from the Jebusites and making it the capital of his kingdom, King David gave the name City of David to the Jebusites' Fortress of Zion.[87] It is mentioned in the Bible forty-three times, mainly in reference to the city's fortress.[88] Gradually, however, the name became synonymous with Jerusalem itself. Over the past 150 years archeologists of various nations have excavated the southeastern hill that slopes down from the Temple Mount, and have confirmed the site's identification with the biblical city, the ancient historical nucleus of Jerusalem. These brief words can hardly do justice to the richness and importance of the findings unearthed over time in the City of David, "the city where everything began." In the area that has been excavated, chapters of the Bible were written, prophets prophesized, and "fateful events occurred whose effects resonate up to the present in cultures of both East and West."[89] Only 160 years ago Jerusalem guides still pointed to the area beside the Jaffa Gate as the place where the biblical events occurred. The archeological research at the City of David, however, has proved beyond doubt that it is the location of the ancient city.

Archeological excavations have been conducted by fourteen different teams under four regimes: Ottoman, British, Jordanian, and Israeli.[90] Their results are spread over tens of thousands of pages in scholarly publications in various languages, and there is hardly space to describe them here. Our focus, in the context of the "Al-Aksa is in danger" libel, is on the excavations at the site since 1967, the era of Israeli rule. These digs have yielded a profusion of fascinating findings that shed new light on the history of ancient Jerusalem and its place in Jewish history and that of other peoples. The most recent discovery is a pair of streets, one running east and the other west, that ascend from the Shiloach Pool northward toward the Temple Mount. Also found under the eastern street was a drainage channel, documented in the writings of Josephus, where the last of the rebels met their deaths when trying to save themselves from the Romans.[91]

These digs, however, have further stoked Muslim criticism and incitement against Israel and its rule in Jerusalem. Again the incitement centers on the supposed danger to Al-Aksa and the Temple Mount compound, ignoring the great distance between the excavations and the mount. Here, too, the inciters deny the Jewish history involved and charge that "the process of damaging Silwan village is not new, as it began at the time when the Al-Aksa Mosque was conceived as a target at the start of the occupation of Jerusalem." As the Ramallah-based *Al-Ayyam* went on to allege in May 2009: "In an initial stage, the area of the Silwan spring [the Silwan tunnel] was Judaized despite the fact that it is a Muslim wakf, and various legends were affixed to it, with Talmudic texts and fabricated claims about a Jewish historical presence and temple in the vicinity."[92]

Two parts of the Herodian street that ascended from the Shiloach Pool toward the Western Wall. The street did not reach the Temple Mount, and its uncovering did not endanger it. (Photos: Vladimir Neichin, courtesy of the City of David, Ancient Jerusalem archive)

The Elad organization's involvement in the excavations began in the early 1990s. Its initiative to set up a visitors center nearby (and receipt of a license to do so from the City of Jerusalem), together with the Antiquities Authority's request that the organization finance rescue digs at the sites designated for development, contributed in no small part to the archeological research at the City of David. Elad's involvement, however, also upped the ante of criticism, since the organization also purchased land and houses in the City of David and populated them with Jews. The criticism made no distinction between political disagreements about the wisdom of this move and Elad's great contribution to the unearthing of Jerusalem's past. Worth noting here are statements of archeologists Prof. Ronny Reich and Eli Shukron, who excavated at the site and were impressed that

> the Elad organization was able to leverage the new and surprising archeological discoveries for the development of tourism in the vicinity…very energetically recruiting funds for continuing the digs and the research, for the preservation and architectural development of the sites unearthed by the digs, and in this regard Elad's activity is without precedent in the history of assistance to archeological research in the city.[93]

The Muslims' Charges: In recent years it has been charged again and again that the digs in the City of David undermine the stability of some of the residences above them. Sheikh Raed Salah and other Muslim elements denounced a plan to excavate the full length of the ancient Herodian stepped-stone street that was discovered on the slope of the City of David. The street ascends from the City of David northward to the southwestern corner of the Western Wall, and continues from there northward along the wall. Muslim critics claim that not only does Israel lack any right to excavate the location or to rule in Jerusalem at all, but, again, they allege that this dig, if carried out, will imperil the Temple Mount mosques. Two petitions[94] were submitted to the Israel Supreme Court in 2008, one against excavating the route of the Herodian-era drainage channel and the second against a dig in the vicinity of the Givati parking lot, which is at the foot of the Dung Gate. The petitioners, Palestinian residents of Silwan, demanded that the court order a group of official Israeli bodies, which had operational and legal authority at the site, to cease their work.[95] In the context of these petitions it was claimed that the digs were being carried out illegally, carelessly, and unprofessionally in a way that jeopardized the stability of the walls of nearby houses. Another accusation was that the excavations constituted the setting of a boundary and an invasion of the petitioners' lands.

The Answer to the Charges: The excavation sites are hundreds of meters distant from the Temple Mount, and the digs pose no danger to either the mount or the mosques. The declared and actual goal of the digs in the City of David is to uncover the location's past as the ancient nucleus of Jerusalem, and to reveal the histories of all the peoples who have ruled Jerusalem as reflected in the relics of the various periods. Nor does the plan to excavate the Herodian stepped-stone street and the drainage channel beneath it, which ascend from the City of David layer to that of the digs at the foot of the Western and Southern walls, affect the stability of the mount. This ancient path links up with a segment of the Herodian street at the southwestern corner of the mount's walls, where it has been exposed and visible for many years. The drainage ditch running under it ascends from the Shiloach Pool to the foot of the Western Wall for a length of some 600 meters. Within the channel were found, along with Second Temple-era coins and cooking utensils, the beautifully preserved sword of a Roman legionnaire, a stone tool with a rare engraving of the Temple's menorah, and a gold earring that may have been sewn onto one of the garments of the Temple priests. At the northern end of the channel, under Robinson's Arch, the original layers of the Western Wall, at their lowest point, were discovered for the first time upon the foundation stone of the mount.

Supreme Court judge Edna Arbel considered the two petitions submitted against two of the City of David excavation sites, and rejected them. In Supreme Court case 9253/08 on the excavations at the Givati parking lot, Arbel wrote:[96] "Many of the petitioners' claims are made nonsubstantively, without presenting any basis for their claims." The judge affirmed that, regarding certain operations connected to the stability of the residences in the vicinity, as described to her by the Israeli professionals who had carried them out, "the petitioners did not present any evidence of the link between the digs and the damages that purportedly were caused to the houses."

Judge Arbel's words on the importance of the digs at the Givati parking lot, which is part of the City of David, are illuminating:

> Apparently there is no disagreement about the fact that the parking lot is located within a national park, and that the excavations performed in it so far have yielded an impressive archeological crop that is of great scientific and historical importance transcending the borders of Israel....This land's rich historical past is enfolded layer upon layer in the earth. The chronicles of the land, of the peoples who have lived in it, have gone beyond the land to enter the pages of history. Over time they were buried in the land and became its hidden secrets.

> "Israel [the judge quoted from another ruling] is indeed a young country, but its roots lie deep in human history, and its land is replete in its length and breadth with relics of an ancient human civilization, which existed and created in this region for thousands of years."[97] This is all the more true concerning the area known as the City of David. The ruins of the City of David tell the tales of Jerusalem for these thousands of years, as we can learn further in the Bible (see, for example, 2 Samuel 4-8; 2 Samuel 9:11; 1 Chronicles 15:1, the place having already been mentioned, of course, in the story of the sacrifice of Isaac) and other sources.

> The importance of the hidden secrets of the City of David is national and international; it is not unique to the Jewish people but, rather, is important for all who seek to investigate the history of the region that is the cradle of the monotheistic religions. The importance of the archeological research is not limited to understanding the land's past and the possibility of examining the accuracy of the details known to us from other sources; it sheds light on the development of human culture. As such, its importance transcends peoples and borders.[98]

Arbel noted that "it was made clear that the excavation work in the parking lot is being done under the supervision and with the accompaniment of professionals."

In Supreme Court case 1308/08 that was submitted against the excavation of the Herodian-era drainage channel in the City of David, Arbel remarked:

> First of all, notwithstanding the claims of the petitioners, it was explained that the work is being carried out with the accompaniment and supervision of professional engineering in the framework of an approved construction plan. And that is not all. As the respondents' statements make clear, most of the activities the Antiquities Authority is conducting at the drainage channel are not actually excavation work, but the removal of trash that has been accumulating there for some two thousand years.

Arbel noted the support and strengthening operations that were carried out to prevent damage, and summed up: "It can be said, then, that the operations are being conducted with the accompaniment and supervision of professionals, notwithstanding the claims of the petitioners." She further asserted: "These professionals are not solely concerned with completing the work on the drainage channel, but also are aware of their obligation to ensure that the work is carried out such that no harm will be caused to the petitioners, their family members, or their property."

As for the property rights of the petitioners, the judge stated that

> insofar as such damage indeed exists it is minor damage….In contradistinction to the damage stands a significant public interest in carrying out the works. Indeed, the uncovering of the secrets of the past, which have lain deep in the earth for hundreds and thousands of years, is a basic element of archeological research. The performance of this work is a multifaceted public interest, given the contribution it makes to the understanding of the history of the land and the history of the Jewish people, and the contribution it makes to the understanding of historical events whose importance is not confined to the Jewish people and their history.[99]

The statements of Prof. Yisrael Finkelstein, one of Israel's senior archeologists, also are worth noting in this context. Indeed, in the past, Finkelstein has advanced the thesis that part of the Bible was written in the Kingdom of Judah in the seventh century BCE; he is not necessarily, then, a reliable historical guide to more ancient periods. He also expressed a reservation about the strong political coloring of the Elad organization, which is managing the City of David. Yet, in April 2011, Finkelstein dismissed the claims that the work in the City of David is illegal or falls short of the standards of modern archeology.[100] In his opinion, the Temple Mount, the City of David, and the southern ridge of the Old City are the location of biblical Jerusalem, and, whatever the political disagreements, the City of David is

> a place of seminal importance for the Jewish people and indeed for anyone who cherishes the heritage of Western civilization….Palestinian accusations—sometimes uncritically accepted by international media—that tunnels are being dug under the Al-Aqsa Mosque in order to undermine its foundations, are false. The closest excavation to the mosque is some 70 meters to its south; this excavation stopped when it reached bedrock.[101]

Cautionary and Safety Measures Taken by Israel: The City of David excavations were carried out with professional supervision, as the above-quoted rulings of Judge Arbel make clear. At two of the excavation sites, subjects of the petitions, the court ordered a halt to the work until a final ruling was pronounced. The excavation of the route of the Herodian drainage channel was halted from March 16, 2008, until the ruling was given on September 21, 2009, a period of a year and a half. In November 2008, because of the lack of a building permit for such operations, an interim injunction was issued against any drilling, digging, building, or casting of columns or retaining walls at the

Givati parking lot. Seven months later, when the City of Jerusalem issued such a permit, the injunction was lifted.

Informal Muslim Attitudes: None have been documented.

Main Archeological Findings:[102]

The Large Stone Structure (Remains of David's Palace?)

In 2005 archeologist Dr. Eilat Mazar discovered remains of a great edifice that was dubbed the Large Stone Structure. Mazar is inclined to identify it with King David's palace, but some disagree with her.[103] Mazar's excavation went beneath the levels of the Byzantine- and Second Temple-era buildings, where large unhewn stones were found that were used for the structure's foundation, its upper parts not having survived. The thickness of the structure's eastern wall reaches 6.5 meters; the length of another wall, north of the area of the dig, comes to over 30 meters. Whether or not this is actually the palace of King David, it is an impressive public building. Also found here were two particularly interesting seal impressions.[104] One carries the name Jehucal ben Shelemiah ben Shevi, known to us as one of the ministers of Zedekiah, the last king of Judah. The second, which was found beside the structure but not within it, carries the name of his fellow official Gedaliah ben Pashur. These two ministers were among the enemies of the prophet Jeremiah and tried to kill him. As Mazar herself writes about the excavation: "The historical description in 2 Samuel 5 of David and his allies the Phoenicians, well-reputed builders who construct for him a new palace, strikingly comports with the facts that have been discovered so far in excavating the Large Stone Structure."[105]

Area G

On this gradient, in various periods, the houses of Jerusalem were built. The archeologist Prof. Yigal Shiloh excavated here from 1978 to 1985. He was preceded by the British excavators Prof. Macalister and his helper Duncan in the 1920s, and Prof. Kathleen Kenyon in the period of Jordanian rule. Shiloh, following in Kenyon's tracks, unearthed the great find of Macalister and Duncan, an enormous terraced structure on which residences and a royal archive were built in First Temple days. Prof. Shiloh believed the structure had served as a gigantic retaining wall for David's fortress, which stood at the top of the gradient. After Shiloh's death, two of his students who examined the pottery fragments at the site assessed that it was indeed a retaining wall for a fortress—namely, the Canaanite-Jebusite Zion Fortress mentioned in the Book of Samuel. The excavations above the structure led Mazar to raise anew the possibility that it dates from First Temple days.[106]

Also discovered in these excavations was the House of Ahiel, and in its ruins pottery fragments with the inscription "for Ahiel." South of the House of Ahiel was found the House of Bullae (that is, of seal impressions), with fifty-one seal impressions on its floor. The building, which served as a royal archive, was destroyed during the Babylonian conquest of Jerusalem in 586 BCE. The collection of signed documents that had been preserved in it was burned, but pieces of the silt of the seal impressions hardened in the fire and were preserved. On the seal impressions survived names such as Shfatiyahu ben Tsafen and Benyahu ben Hoshiyahu, as well as Gemaryahu ben Shafan (a royal scribe) and Azaryahu ben Helkiyahu (a priest during the First Temple era). Out of the fifty-one seal impressions, forty-five bear inscriptions in ancient Hebrew, including the name of the inscription's owner and that of his father.[107] In an adjacent room, which came to be called the Burnt Room, remnants were found of wooden furniture carved in First Temple times that was imported from Syria, adorned with palm-frond patterns.[108]

Warren's Shaft

The Gihon Spring, which flows from the bottom of the eastern slope of the City of David, was the only spring of Jerusalem. Its low location, however, forced the city's protectors to leave it outside the walls and fortify it. In 1867, the British researcher Charles Warren climbed from the Gihon Spring up a vertical shaft more than 13 meters high. At the top of the shaft Warren discovered a winding tunnel that led into the city. For many years the shaft, which ever since has been called Warren's Shaft, was thought to be the main ancient water-supply system, and it was commonly assumed that during sieges water was drawn from the spring via this system.

Since 1995, following Reich and Shukron's excavation, new findings have put the ancient water system in a new light. It turns out that as far back as the eighteenth century BCE, the Canaanites dug a large pool out of rock and surrounded it with fortifications near the Gihon Spring. The city's residents made their way to the fortified pool, which was outside the walls, through a secret tunnel that Warren discovered, and could draw water from it well protected. Only about a thousand years later in the eighth century BCE, the era of the kings of Judea, was the level of the tunnel's floor deepened for an unknown reason. That deepening led to the chance discovery of the natural karstic shaft now known as Warren's Shaft. It appears that this shaft played no role in the original Canaanite water system. Still undecided, though, is the question of whether the shaft became part of the water system after it was discovered.

Fortifications of the Spring and the Canaanite Pool

The "secret tunnel" led to the rock surface of the eastern slope, outside the walls of the city. Here stood a large pool that was dug out of natural rock. It was the focal point of the Canaanite water system, the Canaanites drawing their water from it. This pool, too, was dug in the eighteenth century BCE but went out of use in the eighth century BCE, possibly because of the digging of Hezekiah's Tunnel. A dirt filling was raked into it from the near vicinity, and on this filling homes were built. Fragments of some two hundred seal impressions without inscriptions as well as thousands of fish bones were discovered in the dirt filling, dating from the end of the ninth century BCE.

The Gihon Spring

The ancient Roman arch over the staircase that descends today to the spring, along with other findings, testifies that in Second Temple days, too, the residents of Jerusalem were familiar with the spring. Under the staircase a Second Temple-era *mikveh* was discovered.

The Pool Tower

Giant stones, weighing a few tons each, that were discovered beside the spring constituted the foundations of the Pool Tower that protected the flow system of the Gihon. This marked the first time that building stones of such a size from ancient pre-Herodian eras were unearthed in Jerusalem. The eastern wall of the tower is 7 meters thick, and the tower's area comes to about 230 square meters.

The Canaanite Channel

The channel extends under the Pool Tower for some 400 meters until it reaches a reservoir that stood at the mouth of the valley in the southeastern City of David. The channel's northern segment is covered with giant stones; its southern part is carved in rock as a closed tunnel, but with a kind of open "windows" that served to convey the water for irrigation of the fields.

Hezekiah's Tunnel

The fear that the plentiful water outside the city would serve the Assyrian army haunted Hezekiah, king of Judea. He diverted the Gihon waters to a tunnel that was dug deep into the rock. Known as Hezekiah's Tunnel, it was dug at a lower level than that of the Canaanite channel, making the latter obsolete. The winding tunnel carried the water to the Shiloach Pool in the southwestern City of David. The pool, which had been isolated, was now included within a new wall that Hezekiah built. Known as the Wide Wall, remnants of it were found in the Jewish Quarter. The tunnel was dug in two directions simultaneously at a total length of 533 meters. In 1980, an ancient Hebrew inscription was discovered six meters before the tunnel's opening. It describes how, in the last moments of the complex endeavor of the digging, the two groups of hewers converged.

The Walls of Ancient Jerusalem – Area A

The original wall of the city was discovered in the 1960s by Kenyon. Also discovered in those years was the foundation of a Canaanite tower from the eighteenth century BCE on the southwestern slope of the City of David, and, next to it, a segment of a wall from the eighth century BCE (First Temple period). Further segments of these walls were discovered in 1978-1985, in Area E, by the archeologist Prof. Yigal Shiloh.

The Shiloach Pool

One of the city's ancient reservoirs stood at the mouth of its main valley. The reservoir contained both rainwater and water from the Canaanite channel. In late Second Temple days, the more imposing Shiloach Pool was built at the spot. The water flowed to it through the ancient Hezekiah's Tunnel. The Shiloach Pool is square in shape, and stone staircases descend to it from all directions. Its stone lining conceals an even older pool from Hasmonean days.

The Stepped-Stone Streets

From the Shiloach Pool, a staircase ascends to a spacious plaza. It was on the plaza's northwestern side that a stepped-stone street from late Second Temple days was discovered. This street is paved with large stone slabs and rises northward from the pool. Today's researchers conjecture that pilgrims went up this street to the Temple Mount and the Temple.

The Eastern Stepped-Stone Street

East of the plaza another Second Temple street was found. Under its pavement, broken in several places, was a large drainage channel with complete cooking pots and coins on its floor from the days of the revolt against Rome. The researchers believe that, in the year 70 CE, the last of the rebels took refuge from the Romans in this drainage channel. It was apparently the Romans who made the breaches in the pavement as they searched for those hiding below. "And after the Romans killed some of the people who came out toward them, and took the rest captive, they looked for those hiding in the tunnels, and tore up the ground over them so that all who fell into their hands were given the sword."[109]

The Byzantine Shiloach Pool

After the Second Temple was destroyed, the original Shiloach Pool disappeared under layers of sediment. It was apparently the Byzantine empress Eudocia (fifth century CE) who built a new pool in the vicinity. Parts of it were discovered at the opening of the Shiloach Aqueduct. The pool became part of the Shiloach Church compound.

The Danger to Al-Aksa from Muslim Building Activity in Solomon's Stables

Background: For years Muslims have raised a hue and cry all over the world about Israel's purported aim to level the Temple Mount mosques and build the Third Temple in their stead. As we have seen clearly, the charge is baseless. At the start of the 2000s, however, a real danger emerged of the collapse of the southeastern section of the Temple Mount compound with damage to the Al-Aksa Mosque—as a result of Muslim building activity. While no one accuses the Muslims of seeking to bring down Al-Aksa, the danger that emerged stemmed directly from their building activity at Solomon's Stables in the southeastern corner of the mount. The Muslims denied this and even created obstacles for Israel when it sought to address the danger.

A real danger emerged of the collapse of the southeastern section of the Temple Mount compound with damage to the Al-Aksa Mosque—as a direct result of Muslim building activity at Solomon's Stables.

Solomon's Stables had been considered an underground structure. Recently it became clear, however, that it is an aboveground one, which was buried under thousands of tons of earth sometime after it was built. The structure in its present form was erected in the Ayyubid era (the seventh and eighth centuries), or, in the view of others, in the Fatimid period (the eleventh century) in a location where, in Second Temple days (during Herod's time), there were underground vaults that supported the Temple Mount plaza. When the Crusaders conquered Jerusalem they turned the place into stables for horses, and the fact that they thought the nearby Al-Aksa Mosque had been the palace of King Solomon (or according to another Crusader belief, the Temple of Solomon) explains the name Solomon's Stables. The compartments occupy 80 meters in length and 60 meters in width. The structure features twelve rows of pillars connected by arches.[1]

In 1995-1996, the Israeli Islamic Movement began to renovate Solomon's Stables with the aim of converting it into a mosque. Spokesmen for the movement claimed that in the past Solomon's Stables had served as a prayer hall named after the caliph Marwan, father of Abd al-Malik, the builder of the Dome of the Rock. Hence it was called Al-Masjid al-Marwani (the Marwani Mosque); but the claim has no historical basis.[2] The renovations in the underground compound were done at first without official approval, and sometimes building materials were smuggled onto the Temple Mount within worshippers' clothes. This is no mere procedural or inconsequential matter. It should be noted that *building without permission and supervision at a place of the most sensitive aesthetic, religious, archeological, and historical significance was unacceptable, and so was the lack of an Israeli response. That failure to react to the archeological vandalism and severe damage to antiquities, after the excessive forbearance Israel had shown, confirmed the darkest misgivings.*

Solomon's Stables, which became a mosque. According to engineering reports, the operations undermined the Southern and Eastern walls of the Temple Mount. (courtesy of Dan Bahat)

True, in January 1996 the police granted permission to Muslims to use the stables for prayer during rainy days in the month of Ramadan. Yet no consent was given for an overall renovation, nor for turning the place into a mosque. After the opening of the exit gate from the Hasmonean Channel, the Islamic Movement sharply stepped up its activities and converted the structure, which can accommodate ten thousand, into one of the largest mosques in the history of the Land of Israel.

We will not deal with the circumstances in which the building was carried out and the question of whether it was part of a secret deal between the Israeli government and the Wakf. (Some publications say it was agreed that the Israeli government would open the northern exit gate from the Hasmonean Channel at the end of the Western Wall Tunnel, without disturbances by the Muslims, and in return would provide a permit for turning Solomon's Stables into a mosque.)[3] Nor will we elaborate here on the extensive and tragic damage caused to the Temple Mount's antiquities in 1999. It should be noted, though, that this damage resulted from the digging of a gigantic pit to enable the building of stairs, which would descend underground to the stables' northern row of arches. In consequence, two of these arches became the main entrance gate to the underground mosque. It should also be pointed out that these operations were done without any archeological supervision or documentation by the Antiquities Authority, and with heavy machinery. The endeavor included the removal by trucks in the middle of the night of soil that was replete with archeological items from various periods. The soil was dumped into the Kidron Valley and into the Al-Azariah garbage dump. According to data of the Committee for the Prevention of the Destruction of Antiquities on the Temple Mount,[4] in the course of constructing the gate for the new mosque in the stables, a pit was dug that stretches over an area of about 200 meters and a depth of 12 meters.

In 1999 the Wakf and the Islamic Movement in Israel (northern branch) converted Solomon's Stables into a mosque. During the work an enormous pit dug in the soil of the Temple Mount caused major and irreversible archeological damage. (courtesy of Dan Bahat)

Part of the soil containing archeological findings that the Wakf removed from the large excavation at Solomon's Stables. (courtesy of the City of David, Ancient Jerusalem archive)

Israel's attorney-general at that time, Elyakim Rubinstein, called what had been done "a kick at the history of the Jewish people."[5] The then director-general of the Antiquities Authority, Amir Drori, called it an "archeological crime,"[6] while the authority's archeologist for the Jerusalem region, Jon Zeligman, concluded that the work had greatly damaged archeological research.[7] Yet the Israeli government showed extreme restraint toward what was being perpetrated, indeed to the point of not reacting. Why? Because of the profound political sensitivity of the Temple Mount, and the fact that political talks were then being held with the Palestinians. The government feared that assertive action on the mount would negatively affect those talks. The Palestinians, for their part, not only renovated the underground sections of Solomon's Stables but also, above it, paved thousands of meters of the Temple Mount plaza.[8] Several petitions to the Supreme Court, claiming harm to the antiquities and violations of Israeli planning, building, and antiquities laws, were rejected. The court decided that it was not the appropriate venue to adjudicate these matters, saying this was clearly the role of the political authorities and first and foremost the government itself.

Worth noting in this context are statements of Judge Eliezer Goldberg in Supreme Court case 9474/96:

> The heights of the Temple Mount are not like any other place, and the religious and political dispute over the Temple Mount is different from other disputes on which the court is entrusted to deliver a ruling. The question of how to deal with violations of the law...while taking into account the nature and gravity of this special and sensitive place, is not one for which it would be appropriate for this court to seek a solution.[9]

As for the significance of the Temple Mount soil for the study of Jerusalem and its history, the Temple Mount Sifting Project, which is supervised by archeologists Dr. Gabriel Barkai and Yitzchak Zweig, has revealed numerous minuscule findings, dating from Canaanite and Jebusite days (the third and second millennia BCE) through the early First Temple period and the later kings of Judea (the eighth and seventh centuries BCE), the Second Temple period, and subsequent eras. Among the findings: arrowheads from the army of Nebuchadnezzar, who demolished the First Temple; an inscription (silt impression) from the late First Temple period with preserved letters in ancient Hebrew script, from which the name Galyahu ben Amar was reconstructed; and Hasmonean and Herodian coins.[10]

Right: A Babylonian arrowhead of the kind used by Nebuchadnezzar's army, found in the soil of the Temple Mount.
Left: A pendant in the form of a harp, found in the soil of the Temple Mount. (both photos courtesy of the City of David, Ancient Jerusalem archive)

Teenagers and volunteers at the Temple Mount Sifting Project conducted by the archeologists Dr. Gabi Barkai and Yitzchak Zweig at Emek Tsurim in Jerusalem. (courtesy of the City of David, Ancient Jerusalem archive)

The Crisis of the Possible Collapse of the Southern Wall

At the beginning of 2001, the Antiquities Authority found a sizable swelling of the Southern Wall. According to the authority's measurement, it extended along the wall for 190 meters. The most substantial bulge, to the west of the southeastern corner of the Temple Mount, came to 70 centimeters. Along another 60 meters of the wall the bulge came to 30 centimeters, and otherwise was 10-20 centimeters in size.[11]

The Southern Wall (on the left) and the Eastern Wall (on the right) of the Temple Mount, March 1997. Engineering reports stated that the work on Solomon's Stables undermined their stability. (Avi Ohayon, Government Press Office)

The authority's conservation engineers came to an unequivocal conclusion: the Southern Wall was in immediate danger of collapse. These engineers' initial attempt to enter the Temple Mount, so as to survey the situation from the wall's internal side as well, was prevented by the Israeli authorities because of Muslim opposition. Nor did initial quiet contacts with the Wakf administration and Jordanian officials bear fruit. The mufti of the Temple Mount and Jerusalem, Sheikh Sabri, went so far as to deride "Israel's sanctimoniousness in its concern about the phenomenon and its risks, while purporting to be more concerned about Al-Aksa than the Muslims themselves." He stressed that "the Muslims have been dealing with the phenomenon for four years, in the context of the renovations on the Temple Mount, but the occupation seeks to hamper this renovation activity. The renovation of the mount is the exclusive concern of the Wakf, and the Muslims will not allow anyone outside the Wakf to deal with it." Furthermore: "The Muslims have given their lives in warfare for the mosque, and they will not shrink from further sacrifices for the sake of its renovation." Sheikh Sabri rejected the claim that the damage to the Southern Wall had been caused by the renovations and construction at Solomon's Stables. Instead he blamed the "occupation" and its excavations under and along the wall.[12]

Despite the mufti's words, and the denial of any link between the work on Solomon's Stables and what had happened at the Southern Wall, the professional assessments were clear-cut regarding both the danger of collapse and what was causing it. Although sometimes differing in emphasis, the common denominator of the professional assessments submitted to the Antiquities Authority, intended both for the Committee for the Prevention of Destruction of Antiquities on the Temple Mount and for a Jordanian delegation that came to Israel to inspect the area, was that the swelling had resulted from a change in the flow and seepage regime of the water in the southeastern part of the mount.[13]

From the moment the Muslims paved the Temple Mount plaza, a large part of the rainwater seeped into the Southern Wall, causing it to swell and creating numerous cavities and fissures.

Until Solomon's Stables was cleaned and the plaza above it paved, the rainwater would trickle down to the ancient arches in the stables and from there continue to the foundation stone. But from the moment the Temple Mount plaza was paved, most of the rainwater flowed to the periphery, and a large part of it seeped into the Southern Wall and began causing it to swell. The materials within the stones of the wall's surface were premodern, hundreds of years old with a somewhat claylike composition. This made them swell from any contact with water, which now, thanks to the paving of the mount, was seeping into the wall in great quantities. When the water dried up, the wall's internal material shrank, creating cavities as well as numerous fissures between the wall's surface stones and its internal core.[14]

The engineers were alerted to this dangerous process by trial drills performed at the Southern Wall. Repeated measurements in 2001-2002 revealed that the situation was not static and, indeed, a process was underway. The swelling of the wall was not without effect. In one of the measurements carried out on March 4, 2002, a movement of up to 20 centimeters, compared to the previous measurement, was found at several specific points near the swelling. Hence, in March 2002, the police recommended to both the Wakf and the Israeli government that the southern part of the underground mosque of Solomon's Stables, not far from the swelling, be closed to prevent people from entering it.

The Wakf authorities created many difficult obstacles to dealing with the problem, and contacts with Jordan and other Arab parties were needed to get the Wakf to recognize the severity of the crisis and cooperate in repairing the Southern Wall. Only after it was convinced that there was real danger to the wall's stability did the Wakf accept a proposal that a Jordanian taskforce work with it in tackling the problem. Israel supposedly observed from a distance but, unofficially, was involved in the endeavor. About 200 meters of stone from the front of the wall was removed, its interior in these places was reinforced, and the old stones were replaced with new ones.

The Crisis of the Possible Collapse of the Eastern Wall

In June 2003, Jerusalem district police officers detected signs that the Eastern Wall in the vicinity of Solomon's Stables was leaning sideways in a dangerous way. The Antiquities Authority's inspection led it to conclude that there was a danger of this wall's collapse as well. They also warned that the ceiling of Solomon's Stables, or parts of it, could collapse too.

Compared to the Southern Wall, at the Eastern Wall of the Temple Mount compound the problem was even graver. If the Southern Wall were to collapse, most likely the pillars that support the ceiling of Solomon's Stables, pillars whose direction is north-south, would be exposed to view from the south but would not buckle. But if the Eastern Wall, which also runs north-south, were to collapse, the thirteen pillars, which rest on twelve arcades (composed of eighty-eight piers), would likely fall like a house of cards, one after the other.

The problem of the leaning of the Eastern Wall had long been known. A repair was carried out as far back as 1882. Nevertheless, the problem worsened with time. The building operations in the Solomon's Stables area, particularly the pouring of concrete slabs and the passage of machinery over the roof of the stables, accelerated the process at the Eastern Wall. In July 2003, the engineer Ofer Cohen reported to the director-general of the Antiquities Authority, Shuka Dorfman, that the easternmost wall of the stables, which is its retaining wall, supporting the eastern pillar, was leaning some 40-50 centimeters outward. (Cohen also identified signs of cracking and crumbling in the inner recess of the stables.) In September, Cohen wrote to Dorfman that any damage to the Eastern Wall will probably cause the collapse in a chain reaction of considerable parts of Solomon's Stables. This is because the pillars naturally balance each other's horizontal pressure. If there is damage to the stability of the outermost pillar, there will be nothing to balance the pressure of the rest of the pillars, which will probably lead to their collapse. In case of a mass event, inside and on the roof of the stables, the dimensions of the catastrophe could be very great.[15]

The earthquake in February 2004, which toppled the Mughrabi Gate access ramp, further increased the leaning of the Eastern Wall by 2.5 centimeters. The pressure on the arches, resulting from the greater burden from the plaza above, started a process of the shedding of stone and plaster from the arches. Each morning Wakf members would go down to Solomon's Stables and sweep up the fallen material.[16]

At the end of March 2004, Zeligman and Cohen again warned that "the Eastern Wall is in immediate danger of collapse." They recommended prohibiting entry to the Marwani Mosque and its surroundings until the wall was repaired.[17] The police joined in this demand, fearing that during the days of Ramadan, when tens and sometimes hundreds of thousands visit the mosque and the plaza, the added weight would create an additional stress on the ceiling, which rests on the Eastern Wall, possibly causing a collapse and a severe human calamity.

The Muslims saw things in a different light. They pointed to the results of an inspection by an Egyptian-Jordanian team of experts, which found that there was no danger of collapse at the site. Yet a report by experts of the Haifa Technion contradicted the Egyptian report completely, confirming a danger of immediate collapse.[18] Sometime later it emerged that the Egyptian report was submitted by professionals in building but not in infrastructure and this explained the discrepancy. Yet, even when that was clarified to the Wakf administration, it rejected the information and reiterated that it did not recognize Israeli sovereignty at the location. Having no other choice, the commander of the Jerusalem police district, Ilan Franco, went to Jordan and asked for help from the Jordanian Royal House, but this too was refused.[19] The police then announced to the Wakf that if it did not install engineering support for the Eastern Wall and prevent worship at Solomon's Stables, the number of worshippers permitted to enter the Temple Mount would be restricted, and worship above and in parts of the stables would be prohibited. Again the Wakf rebuffed the demand. The Islamic Movement, for its part, went so far as to call the police warnings "false and malicious" and an "Israeli plot to implement the plans they dream about day and night." The chairman of the United Arab List, Member of Knesset Abd al-Malik Dehamshe, declared: "The mosques are in no danger of collapse, and if the Israeli government intends to prevent worship at them, that will only be to advance its goals of worshipping where some of them stand and destroying the Al-Aksa Mosque."[20]

Only in November 2004 did the Wakf, in cooperation with Jordan, complete the engineering-support operations in line with the requests of the Israeli professionals. They installed support anchors between the Eastern Wall and nine of the pillars in the first row of arches, and additional support anchors between this row of arches and the succeeding arches.

As with the danger to the Southern Wall, regarding the Eastern Wall as well the Israeli legal authorities and professionals had trouble dealing directly with the problem because of the restrictions imposed on them by the government. The Wakf, which toughened its stance, did not make things easier for the government. The heads of the Wakf made clear that they would not allow access to the relevant Israeli actors. Since the Western Wall Tunnel riots in September 1996, the Wakf had barred Antiquities Authority supervisors from entering the closed areas of the Temple Mount even for routine visits. The authority used various stratagems to get around this obstacle, sometimes even disguising archeologists in police uniforms. Only after some years had passed did the Wakf partially lift the restrictions, and today the authority's visits to the site are relatively unimpeded.

The relationship between the government and the Wakf has had to take into account interests that were not always beneficial to the antiquities and to archeology on the Temple Mount. The main interest concerned public well-being and the preservation of order and security at the compound. Another interest concerned relations with the Kingdom of Jordan, which since 1967 had maintained an ongoing connection with the Temple Mount mosques and even won Israel's recognition for its special status. Other countries that were part of this delicate fabric were Egypt, Turkey, and Morocco, as well as the Palestinian Authority.

Nevertheless, when it came to addressing the danger of the collapse of the Southern and Eastern walls, the Israeli authorities acted against almost insurmountable odds. This emerged in a discussion in the Interior and Environmental Quality Committee of the Knesset on May 18, 2004. As Micha Ben-Nun, director of the Licensing and Supervision Department of the City of Jerusalem, explained:

> The City of Jerusalem has formal and statutory authority over the Temple Mount, but in practice we have no control and no access to it. And that's not all. There is also what is called "deliberate obstruction" by the parties that rule the Temple Mount, including the police and so on, denying us access and keeping us in the dark. Any information we receive is unofficial. Even information about the collapse of the Eastern Wall…no one reports to us. No one speaks with us. We have no way to get hold of official information.[21]

Similar statements were made in this discussion by Antiquities Authority director Shuka Dorfman, who admitted that because of a political decree by the prime minister, the authority's supervision of the Temple Mount was at that time partial, indirect, and unofficial. "Lately we have not been there," said Dorfman.

Thus, after almost three and a half decades of the Muslims accusing Israel of plotting and planning to topple the Temple Mount mosques and shake the foundations of the compound, the Muslims themselves created a real danger of the collapse of two of the mount's walls through their work at Solomon's Stables. Yet, instead of immediately acknowledging this, they raised obstacles to treating the problem, denied their responsibility, and stood their ground to the point of endangering the compound and the Muslim worshippers.

The Israeli concern about the unsupervised work in the area of Solomon's Stables was only heightened by the fact that the vicinity of the Al-Aksa Mosque is known to be of weak stability. This was seen when sizable earthquakes struck the Land of Israel and Jerusalem, such as the ones in 1033, 1547, and 1927. These quakes either destroyed the Al-Aksa Mosque or severely damaged it, while the Dome of the Rock almost escaped damage. These two structures were indeed built in the same period, the golden age of the Umayyad Dynasty. Al-Aksa, however, rests on underground recesses that gravely endanger its foundations in case of an earthquake, whereas the Dome of the Rock stands on a foundation stone that is actually the bedrock of the Temple Mount itself.

This concern surfaced in December 2010 in an interview that the Jerusalem district commander of the IDF Home Front Command, Col. Chen Livni, gave to a local Jerusalem paper.[22] The heavy concentration of visitors, not infrequently numbering tens of thousands of people in the southeastern corner of the Temple Mount—a situation that arose only when Solomon's Stables began serving as a mosque—is hardly reassuring to those in charge of the rescue and security forces, and they too have voiced their fears in various internal forums.[23]

Afterword

The "Al-Aksa is in danger" libel essentially resembles the anti-Jewish blood libels originating in the Middle Ages. It is a baseless fabrication that emerged in a religious context, but also has clear-cut political and national components. Many Muslims throughout the world wholeheartedly believe that "Al-Aksa is in danger," that Israel is actually working to destroy the mosques and build the Third Temple in their stead. That, of course, does not attest to the libel's veracity but to the phenomenal success of its agents and disseminators.

Many of these have been aware for years, and are just as aware today, that there is no substance to the libel. But it has served their personal agendas on both the religious and national levels, and so they continue to spread it. And the disseminators of the libel, from the time of Grand Mufti Husseini to the time of Sheikh Salah, do not hesitate to augment it with anti-Semitic motifs and incitement to violence.

This reality requires a complex response to the libel and its disseminators. The fact that the libel has already sparked riots and violent clashes obligates Israeli decision-makers to treat it as a tangible security threat. They should regard it precisely as they regard threats of suicide bombings, rocket launches, or actions against the mosques by Jewish radicals, because the libel is tantamount to a ticking bomb.

This response should not merely involve guidelines for the security forces. It must be translated into practice, both in the legal-criminal and the deterrent realms. Muslim clerics who engage in disseminating the libel must understand that they are liable to pay a severe personal price, including a prolonged prison sentence.

This is not a restriction on freedom of religion, an infringement of democracy, or even a violation of freedom of speech. A democracy has the right to defend itself against hate speech and incitement, against threats of the sort of lethal violence that has already occurred in the past. If Western countries such as the United States and Britain, and Muslim countries such as Saudi Arabia and Egypt, adopt similar measures against threats by clerics and incitement issuing from mosques, then Israel should too.

At the same time, since the libel is already regarded in wide circles as the pure truth, the burden of proof is on Israel as the Jewish state to demonstrate that it is doing everything to prevent harm to the Temple Mount mosques and to allow the continuation of Muslim worship in them.

The information work that is needed is not so complicated. This book provides numerous talking points: from the almost unimaginable concession by one religion of its most sacred site, the Temple Mount, to another religion, Islam, for which the mount is only the third holiest site, through an array of interdictions, arrests, trials, and imprisonments that Israel has exercised against Jewish and Christian radicals who have sought to harm the mosques. This can be compared with the degree of public order, and of freedom of access and worship, provided for sacred sites in the Muslim world, whether in Mecca or Medina in Saudi Arabia, Mashhad or Qom in Iran, or Najaf or Karbala in Iraq.

The agents of the libel are also disseminating factual lies about the excavations at various sites surrounding the Temple Mount and the threats they ostensibly pose. These are for the most part transparent lies that need to be addressed and exposed. The incitement, libel, and violence, the political exploitation of the Temple Mount mosques, their use as staging grounds for terror, the recent Muslim attempt to evade responsibility for the genuine danger created to the Temple Mount compound's stability by work conducted by Muslims (not Jews) in the southeastern part of the mount, in the area of Solomon's Stables—all these are important elements in grasping the overall picture and the motives of the libel's agents and disseminators.

The ancient Greek philosopher Democritus authored one of the oldest known blood libels. He claimed that once every seven years the Jews would seize a non-Jew and sacrifice him at the Temple in Jerusalem, tearing his flesh bit by bit. Democritus' libel was targeted at the Jewish people, their religion, and their Temple.[1] The "Al-Aksa is in danger" libel is also directed against the Jewish people, their religion, and the former site of the Temple—the mount. It is simplistic in that it does not distinguish between the thoughts and plans of Jewish and Christian extremists regarding the Temple Mount mosques, and the historical, religious, and emotional bond of the Jewish people and the State of Israel to the most holy site in Judaism. The libel is also despicable in that it deliberately ignores Israel's and the Jewish religion's tremendous de facto concession to Islam on the mount. Finally, the "Al-Aksa is in danger" libel is dangerous because multitudes of incited Muslims throughout the world blindly accept it. It is hoped that this study will illuminate the reality for them and open their eyes.

Notes

Prologue

1   At present the Fatah movement is part of the Palestinian Authority.

2   A photo of the letter from December 3, 2000, found at Orient House, which in the 1980s and 1990s served as the PLO's headquarters in Jerusalem, was provided to me by Brig.-Gen. (res.) Shalom Harari, who also translated it. Harari, a senior research scholar at the Institute for Counter-Terrorism at the Interdisciplinary Center in Herzliya, also served as Arab affairs adviser at the Defense Ministry and in the Judea and Samaria Command of the IDF, and served in the Military Intelligence research division in military-research and intelligence-gathering capacities.

3   The decree appears in his handwriting on the back of Abu Samra's letter.

4   Hillel Cohen, *Kikar Hashuk Rekah: Aliyatah v'Nefilatah shel Yerushayim Ha'Aravit, 1967-2007* [The Market Square Is Empty: The Rise and Fall of Arab Jerusalem, 1967-2007] (Jerusalem: Jerusalem Institute for Israel Studies, 2007), 112.

5   Yitzchak Reiter, "Hashlishi b'Kedushah, Harishon b'Politika" [Third in Holiness, First in Politics], in Yitzchak Reiter, ed., *Ribonut Ha'el v'Ha'adam* [The Sovereignty of God and Man] (Jerusalem: Jerusalem Institute for Israel Studies, 2001), 155.

6   Ibid. To underline the significance, Reiter adds: "Here Muslim pilgrims sit at the first place in holiness in Islam, yet the real emotion grips them at the mention of Al-Haram al-Sharif in Jerusalem, which is considered the third place in religious importance in Islam."

Chapter 1

Introduction

1   The term "Temple Mount mosques" refers to the Al-Aksa Mosque and the Dome of the Rock, which is not a mosque but is called one. For Muslims, the Temple Mount or the Al-Aksa Compound is called Al-Haram al-Sharif.

2   For example, the conversion of the Dome of the Rock to a Christian church called Templum Domini at the time of the Crusader conquest, and the conversion of St. Anne's Church to a *madrasa* at the time of Saladin's conquest.

3   Six hundred years of Roman and Byzantine rule and subsequently 1300 years of Muslim rule.

4   Plural in the Hebrew original.

5   Or Commission report, Part 4, para. 180.

6   "Dehamshe: Ehiyeh Hashahid Harishon b'Al-Achtsa" [Dehamshe: I Will Be the First Martyr at Al-Aksa], *Ynet*, July 11, 2000.

7   The United Nations Educational, Scientific and Cultural Organization.

Chapter 2

The Israeli Relinquishment of the Temple Mount

1   From the last sentences of the Shmona Esrei prayer in the Siddur, or Jewish prayer book.

2   Nadav Shragai, *Har Hamerivah* [The Temple Mount Conflict] (Jerusalem: Keter, 1995), 23. Former Supreme Court president Meir Shamgar, who served as military advocate general, confirmed this to me personally.

3   Ibid. Former head of Central Command Uzi Narkiss confirmed this to me personally.

4   Ibid., 28-38.

5   Moshe Dayan, *Avnei Derech* [Milestones] (Jerusalem: Idanim, 1976), 13.

6   Shragai, *Har Hamerivah*, 19.

7   In the Machpela Cave, the rooms and the prayer hours were allocated between the Jews and the Muslims and the place serves, up to the present, both as a mosque and as a place of prayer and pilgrimage for Jews.

8   Dayan, *Avnei Derech*, 165, 498.

9   For a detailed discussion of Dayan's decision, its motivations, and its implications, see Shragai, *Har Hamerivah*, 22-27.

10 Ruling of the Jerusalem District Court, June 30, 1976, cited in Shmuel Berkovitz, *Milchamot Hamekomot Hakedushim* [The Wars over the Holy Places] (Jerusalem: Jerusalem Institute and Hed Artsi, 2000), 36-37, 266.

11 The Temple Mount Faithful movement was established after the Six-Day War with the aim of realizing the Jewish right of prayer on the mount and strengthening the manifestations of Jewish sovereignty there. For many years the movement's leading figure has been Gershon Salomon.

12 Supreme Court case 3641/03, ruling of April 28, 2003.

13 Quoted in Shmuel Berkovitz, *Ma Norah Hamakom Hazeh* [How Awesome Is This Place] (Jerusalem: Carta, 2006), 501.

14 According to Halakhah (Jewish law), one who is defiled by the dead is one who has come into contact with dead persons or with people who have been in the proximity of dead persons. In the period of the Temple, it was possible to be purified from defilement by the dead by the ashes of a red heifer, diluted in special water, which were sprinkled on the defiled persons. Today no such Halakhic possibility exists.

15 According to the Halakhic ruling that forbids the entry of Jews to the Temple Mount, the punishment for transgressing the prohibition is *karet* or divine punishment by untimely death.

16 For example, Rabbi Ovadia Yosef, head of the Shas Council of Torah Sages, and Rabbi Yosef Shalom Elyashiv, regarded as the greatest adjudicator in the haredi world.

17 Supreme Court case 4185/90, Piskei Din 47(5) 221, opposite the letters a-b. Cited in Berkovitz, *Ma Norah*, 119.

18 Rabbi Shlomo Aviner, *Shalhevetya: Pirkei Kodesh v'Mikdash* [Flames: On Holiness and the Temple] (Jerusalem: Hotsa'at Hamehaber, 1980), 29. Quoted in Berkovitz, ibid., 119.

19 Nadav Shragai, "Ma Rotseh Hashabak m'Gomah" [What Does the Shin Bet Want from Papyrus], *Israel Hayom*, December 11, 2009.

20 Rabbi Yuval Sherlo, "Hamusar v'Hamikdash" [Morality and the Temple], in *Shabbaton: Alon Lamishpachah Hayehudit*, no. 73, July 13, 2004.

21 In the past the Wakf guards have also prevented Christians from bringing Christian sacred texts or crosses into the mount.

22 According to the police, this policy stems from the fear that the Muslims will see mass visits by Jews on the mount as a provocation, leading to violent acts.

23 Nimrod Luz, "Al-Charam Al-Sharif Basiach Hatsibur Ha'Aravi Falestini b'Yisrael: Zehut, Zikaron Kolektivi v'Darkei Havniyah" [Al-Haram Al-Sharif in the Public Arab Palestinian Discourse in Israel: Identity, Collective Memory and Modes of Construction], Florsheimer Institute for Policy Studies, December 2004, 42-45.

24 For more on this activity against different attempts to cause damage on the mount, see Shragai, *Har Hamerivah*, 85-133.

25 Protection of Holy Places Law 1967, Book of Laws 1967, no. 499, June 28, 1967, p. 75.

Chapter 3

Advocate of the "Al-Aksa Is in Danger" Libel: Grand Mufti Haj Amin al-Husseini

1 On the mufti, see Yehoshua Porat, *M'Mehumot l'Meridah, 1929-1939* [From Riots to Revolt, 1929-1939] (Tel Aviv: Am Oved, 1978); Yehoshua Porat, *Tsmichat Hatnuah Haleumit Hafalestinit 1918-1929* [Growth of the Palestinian National Movement 1918-1929] (Tel Aviv: Am Oved, 1976); Zvi Elpeleg, *Hamufti Hagadol* [The Grand Mufti] (Tel Aviv: Misrad Habitachon, 1989); Yael Admoni, "Ashaf Machak Oto" [The PLO Erased Him], report and interview with Zvi Elpeleg, *Yerushalayim*, March 24, 1989; Haviv Canaan, series of articles in *Ha'aretz* from November 1969 on the Arab aristocracy; and also a series of documents that were taken from the state archives, most of them from files that were prepared at the Foreign Ministry as evidence for the Eichmann trial in 1961: bin 3017, files 21-1א and 21-2א.

2 In Nebi Musa celebrations, thousands of Muslim pilgrims visit the mosque in which, according to Muslim tradition, Moses is buried. Moses, in Islam, is one of the prophets who preceded Muhammad. The Nebi Musa Mosque is located in the Judean Desert about 20 kilometers east of Jerusalem.

3 For more, see Elpeleg, *Hamufti Hagadol*, 12.

4 Shragai, *Har Hamerivah*, 263, 265-266; Elpeleg, ibid., 20-21.

5 Zvi Elpeleg, *M'Nekudat Re'uto shel Hamufti: Ma'amarei Haj Amin al-Husseini Meturgamim v'Mevuarim* [From the

Mufti's Standpoint: The Articles of Haj Amin al-Husseini Translated and Annotated] (Tel Aviv: Moshe Dayan Center and Hebrew University, 1995), 157-158.

6   For more, see Shragai, *Har Hamerivah*, 263-267.

7   Elpeleg, *M'Nekudat Re'uto shel Hamufti*, 101.

8   Shragai, *Har Hamerivah*, 263-267.

9   The Pilgrim of Bordeaux who visited the Land of Israel in 333 CE indeed speaks of a "perforated stone" beside which the Jews prayed and lamented, but its location is not clear. Whereas some say it was the Western Wall, others disagree and point to the southeastern corner of the walls of the Temple Mount as seen from the Mount of Olives, which Jews visited for many generations. See Meir Ben-Dov, Mordechai Naor, and Zeev Aner, *Hakotel* [The Western Wall] (Tel Aviv: Misrad Habitachon, 1981), 61. Midrash Shemot Rabba states in the name of Rabbi Acha in the fourth century: "The Shekhinah never leaves the Western Wall" (2:2). Rabbi Acha meant the western wall of the Temple itself; because this, however, was destroyed whereas the western retaining wall remained in place, over the years the tradition of sanctifying the Western Wall as holy to Jews came to be accepted. See Ben-Dov, Naor, and Aner, ibid., 61-62.

10 Ibid., 62.

11 Berkovitz, *Milchamot*, 109; Ben-Dov, Naor, and Aner, *Hakotel*, 33, 56-57, 62.

12 Berkovitz, ibid., 109.

13 Ben-Dov, Naor, and Aner, 58. Ben-Dov bases his claim on Muslim sources.

14 Yitzchak Reiter believes that the place of the tethering of Al-Buraq moved from the south to the west because of a lack of clarity in the Muslim tradition that describes this act. The tradition tells that the Angel Gabriel tethered Al-Buraq "at the gate of the mosque," that is, at the gate of the mount, but it is not clear where this gate was, and in the past the mount could be entered from both the south and the west.

15 Ben-Zion Dinur et al., *Sefer Toldot Hahaganah* [Book of the History of the Haganah] (Tel Aviv: Maarchot-Misrad Habitachon, 1971), Part 1, 305-306.

16 "Mishpat Hakotel" [Ruling on the Western Wall], report of the International Committee on the Western Wall, Tel Aviv, 1931, p. 61; Uzi Benziman, *Ir l'lo Chomah* [A City without a Wall] (Jerusalem and Tel Aviv: Schocken, 1973), 37-38; Berkovitz, *Milchamot*, 110. My grandfather Rabbi Shlomo Zalman Shragai, who lived at that time, told me the same.

17 Dinur et al., *Sefer Toldot Hahaganah*, 306; Berkovitz, *Milchamot*, 110.

18 For a detailed account, see Dinur et al., ibid., 302-315.

19 *Zichronot David Ben-Gurion* [Memoirs of David Ben-Gurion] (Tel Aviv: Am Oved, 1971), Part א, 341-362; Dinur et al., ibid., 302-315.

20 Shragai, *Har Hamerivah*, 226.

21 Elpeleg, *M'Nekudat Re'uto shel Hamufti*, 159-161.

22 Translated from Hebrew.

23 Elpeleg, 160. Quoted from David Ben-Gurion, *Pegishot im Manhigim Arvi'im* [Meetings with Arab Leaders] (Tel Aviv: Am Oved and Schocken, 1975), 34.

24 Ibid., 161.

25 Yigal Eyal, *Ha'Intifada Harishonah* [The First Intifada] (Tel Aviv: Maarchot, 1998), 323; Haviv Canaan, "Hahusseinim—Shavit sh'Hitnapets" [The Husseinis: A Comet that Shattered], *Ha'aretz*, November 16, 1969.

26 Eyal, ibid., 323.

27 Canaan, "Hahusseinim."

28 State Archives, bin 3017, file 2א: from the mufti's diary, November 9, 1944, translation of document 1306 by the Israel Police in the framework of Bureau 06.

29 State Archives, bin 3149, file 16א: from the words of Hitler in a meeting with Husseini in Berlin, November 28, 1941.

30 State Archives, bin 3017, file 1א: a page from Husseini's diary, March 25, 1944, translation of document 1305.

31 Second letter from April 28, 1942 (translation of document 1302 by Bureau 06 of the Israel Police), State Archives, bin 3017, file 1א.

32 Elpeleg, *Hamufti Hagadol*, 171.

33 Haviv Canaan, "Hamufti Tichnen Misrafot l'Yehudim b'Emek Dotan" [The Mufti Planned Crematoriums for Jews in the Dotan Valley], *Ha'aretz*, March 2, 1970.

Chapter 4

The Muslims Rewrite the History of Jerusalem

1   Reiter, "Hashlishi b'Kedushah," 163.

2   Emmanuel Sivan, *Mitosim Politi'im Aravi'im* [Arab Political Myths] (Tel Aviv: Am Oved, 1988), 102-103.

3   Ibid., 90.

4   Ibid., 97.

5   Ibid., 102.

6   For greater detail, see Shragai, *Har Hamerivah*, 43-44.

7   Ibid., 261-271.

8   Ibid., 320-321.

9   Ibid., 320.

10 This was manifested in the October 2000 riots, in which both Muslim and Christian Israeli Arabs took part. See also ibid., 325.

11 Ibid., 321.

12 Yitzchak Reiter, *M'Yerushalayim l'Meka v'Chazarah* [From Jerusalem to Mecca and Back] (Jerusalem: Jerusalem Institute for Israel Studies, 2005), 18-20.

13   Shragai, *Har Hamerivah*, 263.

14 Meron Benvenisti, *Mul Hachomah Hasgurah* [Facing the Closed Wall] (Jerusalem: Weidenfeld & Nicolson, 1973), 239-240 (quoted from there and from archival material that was left by David Farhi, adviser to Defense Minister Moshe Dayan at that time, who advised Dayan regarding the status quo on the Temple Mount).

15 For an in-depth treatment of Jerusalem's holiness in the Islamic tradition, see Sivan, *Mitosim Politi'im Aravi'im*, 89-90; Chava Lazarus Jaffe, "Kedushat Yerushalayim b'Masoret Ha'Islam" [The Holiness of Jerusalem in the Islamic Tradition], in Eli Shaltiel, ed., *Perakim b'Toldot Yerushalayim Bazman Hehadash* [Chapters of Jerusalem's History in the New Era], memorial volume for Yaakov Herzog (Jerusalem: Yad Ben Zvi and Misrad Habitachon, 1981).

16 Bernard Lewis, *Ha'Aravim Bahistoria* [The Arabs in History] (Tel Aviv: Dvir, 1995), 46.

17 Abu Bakr Muhammad ibn Ahmad Wasiti, *Fada'il al-Bayt al-Muqadass* [A Book Pertaining to the Merits of Jerusalem], ed. and intro. by Isaac Hasson (Jerusalem: Magnes, 1979), 25. Cited in Reiter, *M'Yerushalayim l'Meka*, 27, n. 74.

18 R. J. Z. Werblowsky, "Jerusalem: Holy City of Three Religions," Annual (*Jaarbericht*) of the Dutch Orientalist Society, *Ex Oriente Lux*, no. 23 (1973-1974), Leiden, 1975, 423-439.

19 Lazarus Jaffe, "Kedushat Yerushalayim," 120.

20 Amikam Elad, "Har Habayit Batekufah Hamuslimit Hakedumah" [The Temple Mount in the Ancient Muslim Period], in Reiter, *Ribonut*, 73-77; Lazarus Jaffe, ibid., 120-121.

21 Lazarus Jaffe, ibid., 120-122.

22 Ibid., 122.

23 Dore Gold, *Hamaarchah al Yerushalayim* [The Fight for Jerusalem] (Jerusalem: Yediot Sfarim, 2008), 96 (quotations from Gold's book are translations from the Hebrew edition). See also (cited by Gold) Mohammed Abdul Hameed Al-Khateeb, *Al-Quds: The Place of Jerusalem in Classical Judaic and Islamic Traditions* (London: Ta-Ha, 1998), 120.

24 Ibid.

25 Moshe Sharon, "Haktovet Ha'Aravit Mizman Bniat Kipat Haselah b'Yerushalayim" [The Arabic Inscription from the Time of the Building of the Dome of the Rock in Jerusalem], *Moreshet Derech*, January 1996, 62.

26 Menashe Harel, *Shalosh Hadatot v'Trumatan l'Yerushalayim* [The Three Religions and Their Contribution to Jerusalem] (Sharei Tikvah, Israel: Ariel Center for Policy Research, 2005), 67.

27 Elad, "Har Habayit," 62.

28 Harel, *Shalosh Hadatot*, 66.

29 Reiter, *M'Yerushalayim l'Meka*, 21-23.

30 Ibid., 19. The Muslims claim that the Jebusites were ancient Arabs. For example, members of the Saudi royal house, Palestinian archeologists (such as Dr. Dimitri Baramki), Sheikh Qaradawi (the Sunni Muslim Egyptian leader, considered one of the most important Muslim jurists of his generation), Syrian religious figures, and others all identify the Jebusites as an ancient Arab tribe, which migrated from the Arab Peninsula together with the Canaanites some 3,000 years BCE and thus reached the Land of Israel before the Israelites.

31 Ibid.

32 Reiter, *M'Yerushalayim l'Meka*.

33 Ibid.

34 Ibid.

35 The statements were made in an October 2002 interview. Cited in Luz, "Al-Charam al-Sharif," 28.

36 He said this to me in an unofficial meeting with him during the years I worked as a *Ha'aretz* journalist.

37 From a diary that cabinet minister Dan Meridor wrote during the conference. In the author's possession.

38 Reiter, *M'Yerushalayim l'Meka*, 31.

39 Ibid.

40 Ari Shavit, "Hayom sh'bo Met Hashalom" [The Day Peace Died], interview with then-foreign minister Shlomo Ben-Ami, *Ha'aretz*, September 14, 2001. The information appeared in other publications during that period.

41 Yossi Alpher, "Hahar Kadosh l'Yisraelim Chiloni'im" [The Mount Is Holy to Secular Israelis], bitterlemons.org, no. 20, June 5, 2002.

42 Reiter, *M'Yerushalayim l'Meka*; Berkovitz, *Milchamot*; Shragai, *Har Hamerivah* and many publications in *Ha'aretz*.

43 Reiter, ibid., 33.

44 *Fatwa* from April 28, 2002, Islamic-aqsa-online.net (cited in Reiter, ibid., 40).

45 Cited in Reiter, ibid., 36-37.

46 Ibid.

47 Eilat Mazar, *Hamadrich Hashalem l'Chafirot Har Habayit* [The Complete Guide to the Temple Mount Excavations] (Jerusalem: Shoham, 2000); see, e.g., her statements in the Introduction, 14.

48 Ibid., 39. Mazar told this to Reiter in a conversation.

49 See Nadav Shragai, "B'Mlei'at 4000 Shanah l'Hakamat Al-Aksa" [A Full Four Thousand Years since the Establishment of Al-Aksa], *Ha'aretz*, May 11, 2004; Nadav Shragai, "B'Reshit Hayah Al-Aksa" [In the Beginning There Was Al-Aksa], *Ha'aretz*, November 27, 2005. These two articles were written in connection to the publication of Yitzchak Reiter's studies.

50 Reiter, *M'Yerushalayim l'Meka*, 35.

51 Wasiti, *Fada'il*, quoted from Luz, "Al-Charam al-Sharif," 61.

52 Cited in Berkovitz, *Ma Norah*, 257.

53 Ibid., 36.

54 Berkovitz, *Milchamot*, 110.

55 *Encyclopaedia of Islam* (London, 1971). Cited in ibid., 420.

56 Berkovitz, ibid., 110.

57 Quoted in Berkovitz, *Ma Norah*, 258, based on the first edition of Arf al-Arf's book published in Arabic in 1961 in Amman.

58 In his books: *Kadmoniot Hayehudim* [Antiquities of the Jews], A. Shalit, ed. (Jerusalem: Mossad Bialik, 1944) and Josephus, *Toldot Milchemet Hayehudim* [The Jewish War], L. Ulman, ed. (Jerusalem: Carmel, 2009).

59 See, e.g., Matthew 21.

60 *Ktovot Mesaprot* [Inscriptions Speak] (Catalog no. 100) (Jerusalem: Israel Museum, 1973), 166-167.

61 Josephus, *Toldot Milchemet Hayehudim*, 5, 5, 2, 193-194.

62 Mazar, *Hamadrich Hashalem*, 34; for a survey of further evidence of the existence of the Temple, see Berkovitz, *Milchamot*, 256-261.

63 "L'Rishonah Nechsafah b'Mitcham Har Habayit Sridim Arkiologi'im m'Tekufat Bayit Harishon" [For the First Time Archeological Relics from the First Temple Period Have Been Discovered on the Temple Mount], official announcement of the Antiquities Authority, October 2007.

64 Ibid.

65 Ibid.

66 Dr. Yuval Baruch in a conversation with the author, March 2011.

67 The statements were made to me in the course of my work at *Ha'aretz*.

68 A rescue dig is an archeological dig at an antiquities site that has been harmed, or is likely to be, during development work (paving, building, etc.). The dig is aimed at uncovering the archeological and historical information existing at the site and at salvaging the ancient relics contained therein.

69 An announcement of the Antiquities Authority on September 23, 2009: "L'Rishonah Nechsafah Machtsavah sh'Sipkah Avnei Anak l'Bniat Har Habayit" [For the First Time a Quarry Has Been Discovered That Provided Giant Stones for the Building of the Temple Mount]. The authority's excavation was conducted by Irena Zilberbod. See also Nadav Shragai, "Nechsafah Machtsavah sh'Sipkah Kanireh Avanim l'Bniat Beit Hamikdash Hasheini" [A Quarry Has Been Discovered that Apparently Provided Stones for the Building of the Second Temple], Ha'aretz online, September 23, 2007.

70 A common description, used, for example, by Sheikh Akrama Sabri and Sheikh Raed Salah at media events I attended during 2007-2010.

Chapter 5
Forms of the Libel: Identifying a Country with the Extremism It Fights Against

1 Itamar Marcus and Yaara Piron, "Tamulat Fatach v'Chamas: 'Misgad al-Achtsa b'Sakanah'" [Fatah and Hamas Propaganda: "The Al-Aksa Mosque Is in Danger"], September 9, 2008, Palestinian Media Watch, at: www.palwatch.org.

2 Research report of the Intelligence and Terrorism Information Center (ITIC) on the Muslim Brotherhood movement, March 22, 2011, at: www.terrorism-info.org.il/site/home/default.asp.

3 Akef ended his tenure in 2010.

4 Jonathan Dahoah Halevi, "Ha'Achim Hamuslimim Korim l'Jihad" [The Muslim Brotherhood Calls for Jihad], Machlakah Rishonah website (www.news1.co), August 20, 2006.

5 Gold, Hamaarchah al Yerushalayim, 19.

6 Report of the Intelligence and Terrorism Information Center, "Tasiat Hasinah: Bitui'im Antishemi'im Batikshoret Hayardenit" [The Hate Industry: Anti-Semitic Expressions in the Jordanian Media], April 2005, at: www.terrorism-info.org.il/site/home/default.asp.

7 Al-Dustour, July 4, 2010; see "Cartoons," at: www.palwatch.org.

8 This cartoon was published in the UAE newspaper Al Bayan on July 6, 2010; see "Cartoons," at: www.palwatch.org.

9 The quotation is taken from a report by MEMRI (the Middle East Media Research Institute), which translated the statements from the Egyptian newspaper Al Ahram Al Arabi, www.memri.org, October 28, 2000.

10 Ibid.

11 "Dilegitimatsia shel Yisrael b'Shiluv Mesarim Antishemi'im Basifron sh'Chiber Hasheich Akrama Sabri" [The Delegitimization of Israel in the Various Anti-Semitic Messages in the Booklet Written by Sheikh Akrama Sabri], report of the Intelligence and Terrorism Information Center, November 2003, at: www.terrorism-info.org.il/site/home/default.asp.

12 Al-Balad, July 31, 1997; Al Shav, October 11, 1996 (from a MEMRI report, "Emdot Hafalestinim b'Noseh Hesder Hakeva (1), She'elat Yerushalayim, Merts 1996-Merts 1998" [The Palestinians' Positions on the Issue of the Permanent Settlement (1), the Question of Jerusalem, March 1996-March 1998]), at: www.memri.org.

13 MEMRI report, ibid. From the BBC weekly in English: Al-Mashhad Al-Siyasi, January 4-10, 1997.

14 Al-Hayat al-Jadida, May 22, 2010, from the report "Hachhashat Kiumo shel Beit Hamikdash v'Hazikah Hayehudit l'Yerushalayim" [Denial of the Existence of the Temple and the Jewish Link to Jerusalem], at: www.palwatch.org.

15 Al-Hayat al-Jadida, June 26, 2010, from the report "Hachhashat Kiumo shel Beit Hamikdash v'Hazikah Hayehudit l'Yerushalayim" [Denial of the Existence of the Temple and the Jewish Link to Jerusalem], at: www.palwatch.org.

16 Interview, July 27, 1997, from a MEMRI report, at: www.memri.org.

17 Only once, in January 1976, did a judge in the Shalom Court in Jerusalem, Ruth Ohr, rule in a different spirit when a group of Jews who had prayed on the mount won; however, the District Court invalidated the ruling. For more, see Shragai, Har Hamerivah, 281ff.

18 Voice of Palestine Radio, January 2, 1998, from a MEMRI report, at: www.memri.org.

19 Palestinian TV, August 18, 1997, from a MEMRI report, ibid.

20 Al-Hayat al-Jadida, November 27, 1997, from a MEMRI report, ibid.

21 These three are neighborhoods of Jerusalem.

22 Voice of Palestine Radio, November 26, 1997, from a MEMRI report, at: www.memri.org.

23 Itamar Marcus and Yaara Piron, special study for Palestinian Media Watch on the terror attacks in Jerusalem, September 25, 2008, at: www.palwatch.org.

24 *Al-Hayat al-Jadida*, July 18, 2008.

25 Ibid., August 20, 2008.

26 Ibid., September 1, 2008.

27 See Nadav Shragai, "Cholim al Yerushalayim" [Sick over Jerusalem], *Israel Hayom*, "Israel Hashavua" supplement, December 31, 2010. In the article a former Israel Police commander, retired commissioner Arie Amit, talks about the matter.

28 *Al-Hayat al-Jadida*, May 30, 2008, cited in Marcus and Piron, "Tamulat Fatach v'Chamas."

29 Shragai, *Har Hamerivah*, 29-30; Nadav Shragai, "Rabi Tafsik" [Stop, Rabbi], *Ha'aretz*, December 31, 1997, and also based on a conversation with Rabbi Shlomo Goren.

30 For more, see Shragai, *Har Hamerivah*, Part א.

31 Shragai, *Cholim al Yerushalayim*.

32 Ibid.

33 Shragai, *Har Hamerivah*, 39-46.

34 Ibid., 46.

35 Quoted in Tsvi Zinger, "Har Habayit biyadei Mi?" [The Temple Mount Is in Whose Hands?], *Yediot Acharonot*, "Seven Days," May 20, 1983.

36 Shragai, *Har Hamerivah*. For more on the Goodman affair, see 161-169.

37 That is what, for example, members of the Ateret Cohanim yeshiva in the Old City of Jerusalem did when a disturbed young Jew came to their *beit midrash* (place of Torah study) and there was a concern that he was planning to attack the mosques. See Shragai, "Cholim al Yerushalayim."

38 See, e.g., statements by Member of Knesset Abd Al-Malik Dehamshe in September 2002, quoted in Luz, "Al-Charam al-Sharif," 43. See also statements of the supreme mufti of the Palestinian Authority, Muhammad Hussein, in an announcement to the media from February 7, 2011 (in the author's possession). Hussein accuses the "Israeli occupation authorities" of "granting patronage to the extremist groups" that want to attack the Al-Aksa Mosque.

39 The interview was conducted on January 24, 2001. See Reiter, *M'Yerushalayim l'Meka*, 97.

40 *Al-Asra'a* is the Arabic term for Muhammad's Night Journey to Jerusalem.

41 Reiter, *M'Yerushalayim l'Meka*.

42 Shragai, *Har Hamerivah*, 335.

43 Reiter, *M'Yerushalayim l'Meka*, 102.

44 Ibid., 103. The booklet was published within *Yerushalayim Shelanu: Kovets Hafalot Hinuchiot b'Noseh Yerushalayim* [Our Jerusalem: A Collection of Educational Activities on the Subject of Jerusalem], Society and Youth Administration, Ministry of Education and Culture and Institutes for Jewish Zionist Education (no place, no date), 39.

45 "Emdot Hafalestinim," 23.

46 Reiter, *M'Yerushalayim l'Meka*, 71. The book was written by Dr. Abd al-Salam Mantsur.

47 Statements by Palazzi to the author in one of his visits to Israel.

48 Article by Sari Nusseibeh, in O. Grabar and B. Z. Kedar, *Where Heaven and Earth Meet* (Jerusalem: Yad Ben Zvi, 2010); Shalom Yerushalmi, "Sari Nusseibeh Isher Kium Zikah Yehudit l'Har Habayit" [Sari Nusseibeh Confirmed the Existence of a Jewish Link to the Temple Mount], *nrg-Maariv*, November 27, 2009.

Chapter 6

Sheikh Raed Salah as Successor of the Mufti Haj Amin al-Husseini

1 For more, see Shragai, *Har Hamerivah*, Parts ד and ה.

2 Nadav Shragai, "Hatochnit: L'havi Mi'im Kedushim m'Meka Lahar" [The Plan: To Bring Holy Water from Mecca to the Mount], *Ha'aretz*, November 27, 2001.

3 On the growing ties between the Israeli Arabs and the Arabs of the West Bank, see Shragai, *Har Hamerivah*, 338-339. The Al-Aksa Association for Defense of the Holy Places raises funds and recruits volunteers to protect the Islamic holy places, particularly in Jerusalem, though its official offices are located in Nazareth.

4 Gold, *Hamaarchah al Yerushalayim*, 212.

5   At the time Salah was mayor of Umm al-Fahm.

6   *Yediot Acharonot*, September 21, 1997.

7   Berkovitz, *Ma Norah*, 27.

8   Member of Knesset Abd al-Malik Dehamshe, as quoted in *Ha'aretz*, October 3, 2000.

9   Voice of Israel, March 6, 2001; al-Paluji later denied the assertion, apparently under pressure from Arafat.

10   The commission's official name was the Investigatory Commission on the Clashes between the Security Forces and Israeli Citizens in October 2000.

11   Or Commission report, Part 1, para. 102.

12   Ibid., Part 4, para. 192.

13   Demonstrations against the expansion of IDF training grounds near Arab villages in the Wadi Ara area.

14   Or Commission report, Part 4, para. 179.

15   Plural in the Hebrew original.

16   Or Commission report, Part 4, para. 180.

17   For many years the police station on the mount has stood not far from the Ha-Shalshelet Gate.

18   Or Commission report, Part 4, para. 180. Note that in August 1984 the Wakf demanded the removal of a small Israeli flag the size of a wall picture that hung beside the picture of then-Israeli president Chaim Herzog, in the room of the commander of the police station on the Temple Mount.

19   Or Commission report, Part 4, para. 181.

20   Ibid., para. 182.

21   The commission notes that different speakers defended these calls with explanations expressing profound sentiments of devotion and no intentions whatsoever of bloodshed, but it also notes that "these calls inflame spirits to a level that is not far from mass hysteria," ibid.

22   Or Commission report, Part 4, para. 183. Also based on the "Al-Aksa Is in Danger" supplement of *Tsut al-Chak v'al-Huriya*, September 15, 2000 (no. 3562).

23   In an interview with *Al-Hayat al-Jadida*, August 19, 2000.

24   This is an old structure that, according to activists of the Islamic Movement, served in the past as a mosque. The court rejected this claim.

25   Or Commission report, Part 4, paras. 186-187.

26   Ibid., para. 187.

27   Yoav Stern, Yonatan Lis, and Yuval Yoaz, "Hapraklitut Tivdok im Salah Hesit l'Alimut" [The Prosecution Will Look into whether Salah Incited to Violence], *Ha'aretz* online, February 18, 2007.

28   "Raed Salah: Al-Quds Tihiyeh Bira shel Chalifut Islamit Olamit" [Raed Salah: Jerusalem Will Be the Capital of a World Islamic Caliphate], MEMRI, November 10, 2009, at: www.memri.org.

29   "Haver Knesset Aravi: L'hakim Chalifut Islamit Gedolah sh'Tichlol et Yisrael" [Arab Member of Knesset: Let Us Establish a Great Islamic Caliphate that Will Include Israel], MEMRI, May 9, 2010, at: www.memri.org.

30   Or Commission report, Part 4, para. 172.

31   *Ayyam al-Arab*, July 24, 2000, quoted in ibid.

32   Ibid.; "Dehamshe: Ehiyeh Hashahid Harishon b'Al-Achtsa" [Dehamshe: I Will Be the First Martyr at Al-Aksa], *Ynet*, July 11, 2000.

33   "Dehamshe: Ehiyeh Hashahid Harishon."

34   See Chapter 7.

35   The first direction of prayer in Islam, i.e., Jerusalem.

36   Muhammad al-Dura was the twelve-year-old Palestinian boy whose alleged death from gunfire, as shown in a few seconds of film footage, became a symbol of the Al-Aksa Intifada. Initially various media claimed that he was killed by fire from IDF soldiers, but investigations carried out sometime later revealed that he was shot by Palestinians.

37   *Tsut al-Chak v'al-Huriya*, special supplement published by the northern branch of the Israeli Islamic Movement on January 25, 2000. Quoted in Luz, *Al-Charam al-Sharif*, 33.

Chapter 7

Raed Salah and the Vision of a Global Islamic Caliphate: A Danger to Peace and the Western World

1   The London-based weekly of the Muslim Brotherhood, *Risalat al-Ikhwan* [The Message of Brotherhood], already included in its logo in 2001 the statement: "Our mission: to rule the world." (See Gold, *Hamaarchah al Yerushalayim*, 249.)

2   As summarized by Jonathan Dahoah Halevi, senior researcher and fellow of the Jerusalem Center for Public Affairs. See, e.g., his article "Le'an Choter Salach?" [What Is Salah Aiming For?], *Ynet*, October 11, 2009.

3   From a series of articles that Salah published at the site *Islamic-aqsa*. Quoted by Jonathan Dahoah Halevi in an article from September 17, 2006, on the website of the Jerusalem Center for Public Affairs, www.jcpa.org. Already in 2006, during the Islamic Movement's annual rally in Umm al-Fahm, Salah promised that Al-Aksa and Jerusalem would soon be freed from the hands of the Jews, and Jerusalem would become the capital of the Islamic caliphate.

4   Ibid.

5   L. Barkan, a researcher on Palestinian affairs at MEMRI: "Hatnuah Ha'Islamit b'Yisrael: m'Isuk b'Yerushalayim l'Isuk b'Chlal Hanoseh Hafalestini" [The Islamic Movement in Israel: Shifting the Focus from Jerusalem to the Palestinian Issue as a Whole], August 1, 2010, at: www.memri.org.

6   The *shahada* is the Muslim proclamation of faith, which includes proclaiming the exclusivity of the lord known as Allah and of the divine calling of Muhammad: "There is no god but God, and Muhammad is the messenger of God." Memorizing and reciting the *shahada* is one of the five pillars of Islam—the five basic commandments that are incumbent on every Muslim.

7   Barkan, "Hatnuah Ha'Islamit."

8   See a detailed picture on the *New Islamic Empire* site, www.newislamicempire.com, a compendium of data, analyses, and commentaries on this subject.

9   A detailed description of the Islamization trend on the continent was given in a speech by the chairman of the Freedom Party of the Netherlands, Geert Wilders, in New York at the end of December 2010. (A full text in Hebrew appears at the site www.kivunim.org.) Quoted in the news sections of major websites in Israel and abroad.

10 Ibid.

11 The quotes from Ganaim are from an interview with the weekly *Kul al-Arab* at the beginning of May 2010. See a summary on *Ynet*, May 10, 2010: "Chaver Haknesset Ganaim: L'hakim Chalifut Islamit b'Yisrael" [Member of Knesset Ganaim: An Islamic Caliphate Should Be Set Up in Israel].

12 As he did, for example, in December 2007 when he said his country's policy was part of the Muslim struggle against American hegemony, with the larger aim of establishing a worldwide Islamic caliphate as required by Muhammad. Based on an intelligence investigation by an official source, December 2007. In the author's possession.

13 These statements were made on the Al Jazeera network on November 7, 2000, and are quoted here from MEMRI's translation of November 11, 2000: "Bachir Chechni Matria: Anu Ne'archim l'Peulot neged Hayehudim" [A Senior Chechen Figure Warns: We Are Prepared to Act against the Jews], at: www.memri.org.

14 Jonathan Dahoah Halevi, "Pe'ilutah shel Hatnuah Ha'Islamit l'Chisul Medinat Yisrael" [The Islamic Movement's Push to Destroy the State of Israel], website of the Jerusalem Center for Public Affairs, August 24, 2008, www.jcpa.org.

15 For example, the words of Yunis al-Astal, one of the Hamas leaders, on March 15, 2008, from an intelligence investigation by a security official, March 2008. In the author's possession.

16 Al-Aqsa channel, April 11, 2008. Quoted in a report of the Intelligence and Terrorism Information Center from March 1, 2009, "Shimush Bamisgadim l'Tsrachim Tsvai'im v'Politi'im al-yadei Chamas v'Irgunei Teror Acherim" [Use of the Mosques for Military and Political Purposes by Hamas and Other Terror Organizations], at: www.terrorism-info.org.

17 Meirav Londner, "Yesh Derech Chazarah: Pe'il Hateror sh'Metif l'Shalom" [There Is a Way Back: The Terrorist Who Preaches Peace], *nrg-Maariv*, September 13, 2010.

18 Nasrallah in an interview with the Al-Manar television network, April 1, 2010. From an investigation by an intelligence official, April 2010, in the author's possession.

19 Gold, *Hamaarchah al Yerushalayim*, 221.

20 An interview with the Kuwaiti newspaper *Al Jarida*, June 9, 2008, quoted by Jonathan Dehoah Halevi in an

article on the website of the Jerusalem Center for Public Affairs, June 11, 2008, www.jcpa.org.

21 Nadav Shragai, "Hatra'ot: Miflegah Islamit Metifah m'Yerushalayim l'Hakamat Chalifut" [Warnings: An Islamic Party Is Preaching from Jerusalem on the Establishment of a Caliphate], *Ha'aretz*, November 20, 2006.

22 Gold, *Hamaarchah al Yerushalayim*, 221-223.

23 Ibid., 222-223.

Chapter 8
Terror from the Temple Mount Mosques

1   "Shimush Bamisgadim."

2   Ibid., 36.

3   Ibid., 32-33.

4   Ibid., and see at length in "Shimush Bamisgadim."

5   A report in the evening edition of *Ha'aretz*, July 15, 1938. Quoted in Dotan Goren, "Hazavit Hahistorit l'Tofa'at Hashimush Bamisgadim l'Tsarchim Tsvai'im al-yadai Irgunei Hateror Hafalestini'im" [The Historical Background of the Use of the Mosques for Military Purposes by the Palestinian Terror Organizations], March 16, 2009, Intelligence and Terrorism Information Center, at: www.terrorism-info.org; Rafi Kitron, *Eretz Yisrael Hanisteret: Sipuram shel Haslikim v'Toldoteihem* [The Hidden Land of Israel: The Story of the Secret Weapons Caches and Their History] (Jerusalem: Hotsa'at Ariel, 2010), 77.

6   From a report in the *Times* in those days, quoted in ibid., 79.

7   Archive of the history of the Haganah, 105/152, cited in ibid., 79.

8   Ibid.

9   Nadav Shragai, "Diukano shel Tah Chablani" [Portrait of a Terror Cell], *Ha'aretz* supplement, February 6, 1987.

10 Avinoam Bar-Yosef, "Hachokrim Hufta'u: b'Har Habayit Hukmah Chuliah shel HaJihad Ha'Islami" [The Investigators Were Surprised: On the Temple Mount an Islamic Jihad Gang Was Set Up], *Maariv*, October 24, 1986.

11 Shmuel Mittelman, "Arba'at Chavrei Chamas..." [Four Hamas Members...], *Maariv*, August 11, 1993, 10.

12 Shragai, *Har Hamerivah*, 334-335.

13 The event was held on November 15, 1988. See details in ibid., 336-337.

14 Ibid., 334.

15 For details on the gang members and their arrest, see the report by the Intelligence and Terrorism Information Center from July 20, 2008, at: www.terrorism-info-org. It relies, in turn, on a report of the Shin Bet.

16 From the revised indictment that was served against the two in the Jerusalem District Court on January 16, 2011 (file 1459-01-11).

17 Revised indictment for the determination of a plea bargain against Majid Jubeh in the Jerusalem District Court, January 1, 2011.

18 "Chasifat Tashtiot Teror Tsvai'ot shel Chamas b'Yehudah v'Shomron v'Sikul Pigua Hitabdut b'Yerushalayim" [The Uncovering of Military Terror Infrastructures of Hamas in Judea and Samaria and the Thwarting of a Suicide Attack in Jerusalem], briefing for military correspondents, September 2011, from the website of the Israel Security Agency (Shin Bet-Shabak), www.shabak.gov.il.

19 The PLO organ *Filastin al-Thawra*, May 8, 1988.

20 Shragai, *Har Hamerivah*, 337-338.

21 Ibid., 323.

22 "Shimush Bamisgadim," 16.

23 From an interview with the German news agency, *Al-Quds* online, February 15, 2009. Quoted in ibid., 17.

24 *Ynet*, February 24, 2009.

25 "Shimush Bamisgadim," 25.

26 Ibid., 26.

27 Ibid., 35, reference 43.

28 Ibid., 8, 27.

29 Shragai, *Har Hamerivah*, 297, 349.

30 Kollek's letter to the heads of the Wakf, April 10, 1989.

Chapter 9
The Archeological Digs: Near the Temple Mount and Not Under It

1   Amos Elon, *Yerushalayim: Shiga'on Ladavar* [Jerusalem: An Obsession] (Jerusalem: Domino, 1989), 188-189.

2   Ibid.

3   Conversations with Wakf leaders in the 1980s and 1990s. See also Shragai, *Har Hamerivah*, 223.

4   From a conversation with an archeologist who was a witness to this phenomenon a few years ago.

5   Although the Muslim Wakf is convinced to this day that Getz had institutional backing, the fact that the government appointed an internal investigatory commission on the matter shows otherwise. For a detailed treatment of this complex incident, see Shragai, *Har Hamerivah*, 214-222.

6   Only the group of Reform women known as Women of the Wall prays there, after the Supreme Court rejected their request to pray at the recognized prayer plaza. For more on this topic, see Berkovitz, *Ma Norah*, 504-511.

7   Nir Hasson, "Rashut Ha'atikot Chasfah Edut Arkeologit sh'Me'asheshet et Tiur Yerushalayim b'Mapat Madabah" [The Antiquities Authority Has Found Archeological Evidence that Validates the Portrayal of Jerusalem in the Madaba Map], *Ha'aretz* online, February 10, 2010.

8   Announcement of the Israel Antiquities Authority, February 19, 2010, accompanied by photographs.

9   Announcement to the press by the Israel Antiquities Authority, the City of Jerusalem, and the Moriah Society, November 22, 2010, including an assessment of the finding by Jerusalem district archeologist Yuval Baruch.

10   Announcement of the Israel Antiquities Authority, August 13, 2008, accompanied by photographs.

11   For more, see Benziman, *Ir l'lo Chomah*, 158-167.

12   The information was given to me by an archeologist who worked at the site while Prof. Benjamin Mazar was conducting an excavation there, and was confirmed at the time by an official from the Jerusalem municipality.

13   For more on this affair, see Shragai, *Har Hamerivah*, 142-144.

14   Benvenisti, *Mul Hachomah*, 259. In his book *Ir l'lo Chomah*, Uzi Benziman writes that the Israeli archeological team tried to cover up an alarming report on the perceived danger to the stability of the Southern Wall, but the heads of the team, Mazar and Ben-Dov, convinced the Ministerial Committee on the Holy Places that they were acting responsibly.

15   Shragai, *Har Hamerivah*, 230-231.

16   Ibid.

17   Ibid.

18   The details are drawn from Ronny Reich, Gideon Avni, and Tamar Winter, *Yerushalayim: Madrich l'Gan Ha'arkeologi* (Jerusalem: A Guide to the Archeological Garden) (Jerusalem: Rashut Ha'atikot and Yad Ben Zvi, 1998), 20-35, and also from personal familiarity with the findings as a journalist and from often having examined the site with the excavators.

19   Josephus, *Toldot Milchemet Hayehudim*, 4, 9, 12; Mishnah Sukkah 5:5.

20   The second half of the seventh century and first half of the eighth century CE.

21   Shemot Rabbah 2:2 (in Judaism the Shekhinah is the presence of God, especially in the Temple). Yalkut Shimoni (Kings 1:8, section 195) offers a similar statement but calls it the Western Wall "of the Temple." The archeologist Meir Ben-Dov notes that it is because the western wall of the Temple was destroyed, while the western retaining wall was left standing, that over the years the tradition of sanctifying the familiar Western Wall emerged; see Ben-Dov, Naor, and Aner, *Hakotel*, 61.

22   Shragai, *Har Hamerivah*, 227-229.

23   The details are drawn from Reich, Avni, and Winter, *Yerushalayim*, 20-35; Dan Bahat, *Minharot Hakotel Hamaravi* [The Western Wall Tunnel] (Jerusalem: Hakeren l'Moreshet Hakotel Hamaravi, 2003); and also from my personal familiarity with the findings as a journalist and from often having examined the site with the excavators.

24   Bahat, ibid., 29-30.

25   Shragai, *Har Hamerivah*, 233-236.

26   Ibid., 232-236.

27   This information is based on talks with engineers of the Western Wall Heritage Foundation and with other professionals, including members of the Antiquities Authority; visits to the recesses of the Western Wall Tunnel over the years; and study of the files of the Western Wall Heritage Foundation.

28 Summary of the meeting of the Directors-General Forum for Jerusalem Holy Places Affairs, March 10, 1989.

29 Protocol recorded by Ovadia Danon, one of those who took part in the tour; and a conversation with another participant.

30 Conversation with Western Wall Rabbi Shmuel Rabinovich, winter 2010.

31 The information is mainly based on Bahat, *Minharot*, with updates for findings from new excavations (2010) at the site.

32 For many years Bahat was the Antiquities Authority official in charge of work carried out by the Religious Affairs Ministry at the Western Wall Tunnel.

33 From a visit to the site in August 2011.

34 Data of the Western Wall Heritage Foundation.

35 Information is from *Ha'aretz*, September 25-26, 1996. For example, Sami Sokol, "Arafat Koreh…" [Arafat Calls…], September 25, 1996.

36 Guy Bechor, "Nasi Mitsri'im Doresh…" [The Egyptian President Demands…], *Ha'aretz*, September 27, 1996.

37 Berkovitz, *Milchamot*, 77-78.

38 Bahat, *Minharot*, 42.

39 Ibid., 80.

40 Shragai, *Har Hamerivah*, 239; Dan Bahat, "Ta'alat Hami'im Hachashmona'it liyad Har Habayit" [The Hasmonean Aqueduct beside the Temple Mount], *Ariel* (57-58), 1988, 140; Bahat, *Minharot*, 138-157.

41 "Ohel Yitzchak: Choveret Meidah v'Netunim" [Ohel Yitzchak: Information and Data Booklet], Western Wall Heritage Foundation, 2008.

42 Quoted in Ro'i Nachmias and Anat Shalev, "Chafirot Machshidot b'Har Habayit" [Suspicious Excavations on the Temple Mount], *Ynet*, January 21, 2007.

43 Information is based on technical specifications from March 31, 2009, submitted by engineers of the Western Wall Heritage Foundation to their supervisors.

44 Based on a visit to the area as well as explanations from the Antiquities Authority; also on Chaim Baraba and Tawfik Da'adla, "Yerushalayim, Beit Haknesset Ohel Yitzchak" [Jerusalem: The Ohel Yitzchak Synagogue], *Chadashot Arkeologiot* 119, 2007.

45 The cardo was a north-south oriented street in Roman cities and other communities.

46 Nadav Shragai, "Herzl Biker Bo, Harav Kook Hitpalel Bo, Hayardenim Potsetsu Oto" [Herzl Visited It, Rabbi Kook Prayed at It, the Jordanians Blew It Up], *Ha'aretz*, December 19, 2005; "Shichzur v'Bniat Churvat Rabi Yehuda Chasid" [Reconstruction and Building of the Hurva Synagogue of Rabbi Yehuda Chasid], booklet published by the Society for Renovation and Development of the Jewish Quarter, Jerusalem, December 2001; Reuven Gafni, Arie Morgenstern, and David Cassuto, eds., *Hachurvah: Shesh Meot Shanah shel Hityashvut Yehudit b'Yerushalayim* [The Hurva Synagogue: Six Hundred Years of Jewish Settlement in Jerusalem] (Jerusalem: Yad Ben Zvi and the Society for Renovation and Development of the Jewish Quarter, 2010).

47 Mordechai Naor, ed., *Harova Hayehudi ba'Ir Ha'Atikah shel Yerushalayim* [The Jewish Quarter in the Old City of Jerusalem] (Jerusalem: Yediot Acharonot, 1987), 262.

48 The statements were made on the program "With the Events" (*Ma al-Hadat*), Palestinian television, March 14, 2010; from a translation by Palestinian Media Watch, at: www.palwatch.org.

49 The documentary film *Batei Knesset Makifim et Al-Aksa* [Synagogues Surround Al-Aksa], Palestinian television, March 16, 2010; from a translation by Palestinian Media Watch, at: www.palwatch.org.

50 The statements were made on the *Boker Tov Yerushalayim* [Good Morning Jerusalem] program on Palestinian television, March 14, 2010; from a report of Palestinian Media Watch, at: www.palwatch.org.il.

51 *Al-Hayat al-Jadida*, March 28, 2010, 13; from a report of Palestinian Media Watch, at: www.palwatch.org.

52 "Chadashot Hateror v'Hasichsuch Ha'Yisraeli-Falestini" [News of Terrorism and the Israeli-Palestinian Conflict], March 1-16, 2010, Intelligence and Terrorism Information Center, at: www.terrorism-info.org.

53 Ibid.

54 Hearsay evidence made available to me.

55 Arie Morgenstern, "Binian Hachurvah: Ethaltah d'Geulah" [The Building of Hurva: The Beginning of Redemption], in Gafni, Morgenstern, and Cassuto, *Hachurvah*, 84-88.

56 Yair Paz, "Hachevrah bi'Tkufat Hamandat: Chevrah Zikaron v'Semel" [The Society in the Mandate Period: Society, Memory, and Symbol], in Gafni, Morgenstern, and Cassuto, *Hachurvah*, 167-168. The article considers,

among other things, why the Jordanian regime destroyed the Hurva.

57 A report of Palestinian Media Watch from March 2010, which includes a photograph of the cartoon, at: www.palwatch.org.

58 Ibid.

59 Until the Mughrabi Quarter was evacuated, the Western Wall plaza was no more than a narrow alley 28 meters long and only 3.60 meters wide. The website of the Western Wall Heritage Foundation notes that

> the crowding was extreme and for the Shavuot holiday, a few days after the liberation of Jerusalem, there was fear lest the plaza be too narrow to contain the masses of Jews who would come to visit Jerusalem. Col. Shlomo "Cheech" Lahat, governor of Jerusalem and later mayor of Tel Aviv, and his deputy Lt. Col. Albek proposed to the civil authorities that the Mughrabi Quarter be destroyed to make way for a large prayer plaza. Teddy Kollek, mayor of Jerusalem, convinced the contractors organization to do the job, and on a voluntary basis Jerusalem contractors destroyed the houses of the Mughrabi Quarter (their residents were evacuated with their consent to alternative housing) and prepared a plaza to accommodate the worshippers. The evacuation endeavor was supervised by the engineering commander Capt. Eitan Ben Moshe.

For further details on the destruction and evacuation of the Mughrabi Quarter, see Benziman, *Ir l'lo Chomah*, 37-44.

60 The details are drawn from information that was obtained from the Israel Police and the Western Wall Heritage Foundation, and from following what has been happening at the site for many years.

61 The description is drawn from a visit to the place the next day as part of my work as a *Ha'aretz* journalist at that time.

62 The organization's declared purpose is "stability, equality and a political future in Jerusalem." It is identified with the Israeli left and favors a division of the city.

63 The description of this episode is taken from a letter by architect Eli Eilan to Mordechai Eliav, director-general of the Western Wall Heritage Foundation, dated June 11, 2009, and also is based on following the different stages of this affair.

64 According to a source in the Prime Minister's Office.

65 The permit was issued on March 1, 2011.

66 Al Jazeera television network, February 4, 2007. From a report of the Intelligence and Terrorism Information Center, February 7, 2007, at: www.terrorism-info.org.

67 Report of the Intelligence and Terrorism Information Center, at: www.terrorism-info.org.

68 Ibid.

69 Ibid.

70 Ibid.

71 Ibid.

72 Ibid., February 15, 2007. The report surveys the "hate industry" in the Syrian media at that time.

73 Lilach Shuval, "Hamecha'ah b'Yerushalayim: Meot Mafginim mul Sha'ar Shechem" [The Protest in Jerusalem: Hundreds Demonstrate at the Nablus Gate], *Ynet*, February 8, 2007.

74 Ibid.

75 The discovery of this gate was publicized in 1858 by the missionary Dr. James Thomas Berkeley.

76 Masechet Midot, Part 1, Mishnah 3.

77 As he observed in a report on February 11, 2007, which was prepared by the Knesset's Information and Research Center on the work at Maaleh Hamughrabim, for a discussion of the issue in the Knesset Interior Committee.

78 Yuval Baruch, "Maaleh Hamughrabim—Hasipur Ha'amiti" [Maaleh Hamughrabim: The Real Story], an article on the website of the Antiquities Authority, www.antiquities.org.il. Baruch writes further there:

> The first link between Al-Buraq and this vicinity can be credited to Mujir al-Din, a Jerusalem judge of the fifteenth century whose work on "The History of Jerusalem and Hebron" is an important, unique contribution to the knowledge of Jerusalem. Among the structures that he describes in the Temple Mount vicinity is also the mosque known as the Western Mosque: "in the courtyard of the Temple Mount, west of the Al-Aksa Mosque, is a building covered by domes that is known by the name 'the Western Mosque.' This is a place that arouses awe and many come to it to pray." This description shows clearly that at least in the fifteenth century the mosque was located within the Temple Mount plaza and certainly was not part of the area where the Mughrabi Quarter, which also is mentioned by Mujir al-Din, was built.

79 In the author's possession.

80 www.unesco.org/bpi/pdf/jerusalem_report_en.pdf, cited in "The Struggle over the Mughrabi Bridge," an opinion submitted to the government during the crisis by attorney Dr. Shmuel Berkovitz.

81 Ibid. For more, see Nadav Shragai, "The Mughrabi Gate to the Temple Mount in Jerusalem: The Urgent Need for a Permanent Access Bridge," website of the Jerusalem Center for Public Affairs, www.jcpa.org.

82 Ibid., p. 7 of the opinion.

83 A similar readiness to position cameras, which would refute the Muslims' suspicions, was expressed by Reuven Pinski, director of development of the Old City Basin for the Jerusalem Development Authority, in the context of a comprehensive program for renovation and preservation of the Old City. See Pinksi's statements in Eli Oshorov, "Harova Hamuslimi: Ha'iriah Rotsah Lachpor, Hatoshavim Choshashim m'Konspiratsia" [The Muslim Quarter: The Municipality Wants to Excavate, the Residents Fear a Conspiracy], nrg-Maariv, May 12, 2010.

84 Conversation in June 2011 with retired commissioner Mickey Levy, former commander of the Jerusalem Police, and with attorney Dr. Shmuel Berkovitz.

85 Eshkol's letter to the Western Wall Heritage Foundation, May 22, 2011, in the author's possession; Shalom Yerushalmi, "Gesher Hagehenom: Hakrav al Haderech l'Har Habayit" [The Bridge of Hell: The Battle over Access to the Temple Mount], nrg-Maariv, March 11, 2011.

86 Chaim Baraba, Penny Vito, and John Zeligman, "Chafirat Maaleh Sha'ar Hamughrabim" [The Excavation of the Maaleh Hamughrabim Gate], archeological report, January-July 2007. Courtesy of the Western Wall Heritage Foundation.

87 Gabriel Barkai, "Ir David—Milon Musagim" [The City of David: A Primer], in Eyal Meron, ed., Mechkarei Ir David v'Yerushalayim Hakedumah [Studies on the City of David and Ancient Jerusalem], proceedings of the seventh conference of the Megalim Institute, Jerusalem, 2006.

88 Ibid.

89 Eyal Meron, in the introduction to Aharon Hurvitz, Megalim et Ir David [Discovering the City of David] (Jerusalem: Megalim Institute, 2009).

90 Ronny Reich and Eli Shukron, "Toldot Hachafirot Ha'arkiologiot b'Ir David (1867-2007)" [The History of Archeological Excavations in the City of David (1867-2007)], in Eyal Meron, ed., Mechkarei Ir David v'Yerushalayim Hakedumah [Studies on the City of David and Ancient Jerusalem], proceedings of the ninth conference of the Megalim Institute, Jerusalem, 2008.

91 See below, and also in Aharon Hurvitz, Ir David—Sipurah shel Yerushalayim Hakedumah [The City of David: The Story of Ancient Jerusalem], ed. Eyal Meron (Jerusalem: Megalim Institute, 2010), 206-211.

92 Al-Ayyam, May 19, 2009, in a report of Palestinian Media Watch: "Hachchashat Kiumo shel Beit Hamikdash v'Hazikah Hayehudit l'Yerushalayim" [Denial of the Existence of the Temple and the Jewish Link to Jerusalem], at: www.palwatch.org.

93 Reich and Shukron, "Toldot Hachafirot," 30.

94 Supreme Court case 1308/08 and Supreme Court case 9253/08.

95 The petition concerning the Herodian drainage channel was submitted against the Antiquities Authority, the National Parks Authority, and the Society for the Development of East Jerusalem. The petition against the project at the Givati parking lot was also submitted against the City of Jerusalem, Elad, and two entrepreneurs who were involved.

96 Also written in the name of Judges Edmund Levy and Yochanan Meltzer.

97 Supreme Court case: Al-Aksa Society for the Development of the Muslim Wakf Properties Ltd. v. Kerem Maharal Moshav Ovdim l'Hityashvut Shitufit Ltd. (not published, June 17, 2009), and see para. 34.

98 The judge further gained the impression that "the sides...sought to drag the court into the morass of their dispute, which is much wider and more complex than the matter of the Givati parking lot and is not an issue for the court to respond to."

99 Also party to this ruling were the deputy-president of the Supreme Court, Judge Eliezer Rivlin, and Judge Edmund Eliyahu Levy.

100 Finkelstein addressed the issue in his article on the City of David in the Jewish Daily Forward, April 26, 2011, at: www.forward.com.

101 Ibid.

102 For an exhaustive compilation of the findings from all of the periods, see Reich and Shukron, "Toldot Hachafirot." The overview of the main findings of the excavations in the City of David and its vicinity is derived from Hurvitz, *Ir David*; background material for guides in the City of David; Reich, Avni, and Winter, *Yerushalayim*, 44-84; and from Eilat Mazar, *Armon Hamelech David – Pirsum Onot 2005-7* [King David's Palace: Findings for 2005-2007] (Jerusalem: Shoham, 2009).

103 Hurvitz, *Ir David*, 28-30; Mazar, ibid.

104 These were impressions made on silt that served as signatures for documents.

105 Mazar, *Armon Hamelech David*, back cover of the book.

106 Hurvitz, *Ir David*, 34.

107 Ibid., 38; Reich, Avni, and Winter, *Yerushalayim*, 53.

108 Hurvitz, *Ir David*, 37.

109 Josephus, *Toldot Milchemet Hayehudim*, 6, 9, 4.

Chapter 10
The Danger to Al-Aksa from Muslim Building Activity in Solomon's Stables

1 Dan Bahat (with Chaim Rubinstein), *Atlas Carta Hagadol l'Toldot Yerushalayim* [The Great Carta Atlas of Jerusalem History] (Jerusalem: Carta, 2000), 91; Eilat Mazar, *Hamadrich Hashalem l'Chafirot Har Habayit* [The Complete Guide to the Temple Mount Excavations] (Jerusalem: Shoham, 2000), 90; visits to the place over the years in the context of journalistic and research work, and conversations with researchers on the significance of the new findings contained in the Wakf excavations on the Temple Mount.

2 Berkovitz, *Milchamot*, 103. Berkovitz notes there the prevailing view that the chambers served as storerooms until the Crusader period. They then also served as stables, and subsequently were not used at all; see ibid., 451, reference 245. Also Luz, in "Al-Charam al-Sharif," points out that there is no mention of this name in the ancient Muslim sources and that "its choice suggests more than anything else the desire of persons in the Islamic Movement to find a sufficient legitimate and historical basis for the new reality that was created at the compound" (15).

3 For elaboration, see Berkovitz, ibid., 74-77. Berkovitz reaches the conclusion that there was no deal.

4 An Israeli public committee with members from across the political spectrum such as former Supreme Court president Meir Shamgar, former Mossad chief Meir Dagan, former Jerusalem mayor Teddy Kollek, the writers A. B. Yehoshua, Amos Oz, and S. Yizhar, and well-known archeologists.

5 From a source who participated in a meeting where these statements were made.

6 Ibid.

7 Online version of a background document on the excavations on the Temple Mount, Knesset Research and Information Center, November 19, 2001, p. 2, para. 1.7.

8 Many other areas of the compound were paved at the time as well.

9 In Supreme Court case 8666/99, which addressed the Temple Mount Faithful's petition against the state to halt the excavations, destruction, and building on the mount, the Jerusalem police commander stated that "given past experience and the special status of the Temple Mount, unilateral acts by the authorities at the present time [January 2000] that will restore the situation to what it was...are liable to lead—at a level of near-certainty—to bloodshed, outbreaks, and agitation that will boil over from the Temple Mount to Jerusalem, Judea and Samaria, and the State of Israel as a whole." The Supreme Court accepted this assessment.

10 For more on the findings of the Temple Mount Sifting Project, see Gabriel Barkai and Yitzchak Zweig, "Proyekt Sinun Afar m'Har Habayit—Doch Rishoni" [The Temple Mount Sifting Project: A Preliminary Report], *Hidushim b'Cheker Yerushalayim* 11, 2009, 213-217; Nadav Shragai, "Sinun Afar Chasaf Mimtsa'im m'Tkufat Bayit Rishon" [The Sifting of Earth Has Revealed Findings from the First Temple Period], *Ha'aretz*, October 19, 2006.

11 Nadav Shragai, "Rashut Ha'atikot Me'asheret: Sakanah Miyadit l'Hitmotetut Hakotel Hadromi" [The Antiquities Authority Confirms: An Immediate Danger of the Southern Wall's Collapse], *Ha'aretz*, August, 28, 2002.

12 Sheikh Sabri in a speech he gave on August 24, 2001. It was broadcast on the *Mabat* program of Israel's Channel 1 television.

13 Reports of the Israel Antiquities Authority from 2001-2003, reports of the Committee for the Prevention of the Destruction of Antiquities on the Temple Mount from the same period, and details of the report of the Jordanian team that visited the site were made available to me.

14 The process is described in reports of the Antiquities Authority that I have seen.

15 Ibid.

16 According to a police source.

17 Itamar Eichner, "Hakotel Hamizrachi b'Sakanat Hitmotetut" [The Eastern Wall Is in Danger of Collapse], *Yediot Acharonot*, April 1, 2004.

18 Berkovitz, *Ma Norah*, 413.

19 Ibid.

20 *Ha'aretz*, September 27, 2004, quoted in ibid.

21 Ibid., 403.

22 Itamar Fleishman, "Yihiyu Krisot b'Har Habayit" [There Will Be Collapses on the Temple Mount], *Yediot Acharonot*, December 3, 2010.

23 Based on my unofficial conversations with relevant officials in March 2011.

Afterword

1 David Flusser, "Motzeh Alilot Hadam" [The Origin of the Blood Libels], *Mahani'im* 109, 1967.

Index

Note: Some values that appear often in the book were not included in the index: Al-Aksa, Land of Israel, the Temple, the Temple Mount, Israel, the mufti, Palestine-Palestinians, Arabs, and Jewish Quarter. For organizations, political parties, and institutions, several prominent values were included such as: Wakf, Supreme Muslim Council, Israeli Islamic Movement, Antiquities Authority, Palestinian Authority, and Muslim Brotherhood.

About the Author

Nadav Shragai is a senior researcher at the Jerusalem Center for Public Affairs. He served as a journalist and commentator at *Ha'aretz* between 1983 and 2009, is currently a journalist and commentator at *Israel Hayom*, and has documented the dispute over Jerusalem for thirty years.

His books include: *At the Crossroads: The Story of Rachel's Tomb* (Gates for Jerusalem Studies, 2005); *The Temple Mount Conflict* (Keter, 1995); and the essay: "Jerusalem Is Not the Problem, It Is the Solution," in *Mr. Prime Minister: Jerusalem*, Moshe Amirav, ed. (Carmel and Florsheimer Institute, 2005).

More Jerusalem Center Publications on Jerusalem

By Nadav Shragai

The Mughrabi Gate to the Temple Mount in Jerusalem: - The Urgent Need for a Permanent Access Bridge (2011)

Demography, Geopolitics, and the Future of Israel's Capital: Jerusalem's Proposed Master Plan (2010)

Israeli Rights in Jerusalem: The City of David and Archeological Sites (2009)

The U.S.-Israeli Dispute over Building in Jerusalem: - The Sheikh Jarrah-Shimon HaTzadik Neighborhood (2009)

Protecting the Contiguity of Israel: The E-1 Area and the Link Between Jerusalem and Maale Adumim (2009)

The Mount of Olives in Jerusalem: Why Continued Israeli Control Is Vital (2009)

Jerusalem: The Dangers of Division - An Alternative to Separation from the Arab Neighborhoods (2008)

New Damage to Antiquities on the Temple Mount (2008)

The Palestinian Authority and the Jewish Holy Sites in the West Bank: Rachel's Tomb as a Test Case (2007)

By Dore Gold

Jerusalem in International Diplomacy (2001)

Europe Seeks to Divide Jerusalem (2009)

The Struggle for Jerusalem (2009)

See also *The Fight for Jerusalem: Radical Islam, the West, and the Future of the Holy City* (Washington, D.C.: Regnery, 2007)

The Jerusalem Center for Public Affairs is a leading independent research institute specializing in public diplomacy and foreign policy. Founded in 1976, the Center has produced hundreds of studies and initiatives by leading experts on a wide range of strategic topics. Dr. Dore Gold, Israel's former ambassador to the UN, has headed the Jerusalem Center since 2000.

Jerusalem Center Programs:

Global Law Forum – A ground-breaking program that undertakes studies and advances policy initiatives to protect Israel's legal rights in its conflict with the Palestinians, the Arab world, and radical Islam. (www.globallawforum.org)

Defensible Borders Initiative – A major security and public diplomacy initiative that analyzes current terror threats and Israel's corresponding territorial requirements, particularly in the strategically vital West Bank, that Israel must maintain to fulfill its existential security and defense needs. (www.defensibleborders.org)

Jerusalem in International Diplomacy – Dr. Dore Gold analyzes the legal and historic rights of Israel in Jerusalem and exposes the dangers of compromise that will unleash a new *jihadist* momentum in his book *The Fight for Jerusalem: Radical Islam, the West, and the Future of the Holy City* (Regnery, 2007). Adv. Justus Reid Weiner looks at *Illegal Construction in Jerusalem: A Variation on an Alarming Global Phenomenon* (2003). Researcher Nadav Shragai assesses the imminent security threats to Israel's capital resulting from its potential division, and offers alternative strategies for managing Jerusalem's demographic challenge in his monograph *Jerusalem: The Dangers of Division* (2008).

Iran and the Threats to the West – Preparation of a legal document jointly with leading Israeli and international scholars and public personalities on the initiation of legal proceedings against Iranian President Mahmoud Ahmadinejad for incitement to commit genocide and participate in genocide. This program also features major policy studies by security and academic experts on Iran's use of terror proxies and allies in the regime's war against the West and its race for regional supremacy.

Institute for Contemporary Affairs (ICA) – A diplomacy program, founded in 2002 jointly with the Wechsler Family Foundation, that presents Israel's case on current issues through high-level briefings by government and military leaders to the foreign diplomatic corps and foreign press, as well as production and dissemination of information materials.

Combating Delegitimization – A major multilingual public diplomacy program exposing those forces that are questioning Israel's very legitimacy, while carrying out initiatives to strengthen Israel's fundamental right to security and to reinforce the historical connection between the Jewish people and their historical homeland including Jerusalem. The program also provides resources for commentators and educates students to effectively communicate these messages to promote attitude change in targeted populations.

Anti-Semitism After the Holocaust – Initiated and directed by Dr. Manfred Gerstenfeld, this program includes conferences, seminars, and publications discussing restitution, the academic boycott, Holocaust denial, and anti-Semitism in the Arab world, European countries, and the post-Soviet states. (www.jewishaffairs.org)

Jerusalem Center Serial Publications:

Jerusalem Viewpoints – providing in-depth analysis of changing events in Israel and the Middle East since 1977.

Jerusalem Issue Briefs – insider briefings by top-level Israeli government officials, military experts, and academics, as part of the Center's Institute for Contemporary Affairs.

Daily Alert – a daily digest of hyperlinked news and commentary on Israel and the Middle East from the world and Israeli press.

Post-Holocaust and Anti-Semitism – a monthly publication examining anti-Semitism after the Holocaust.

Jewish Political Studies Review – a scholarly journal founded in 1989.

Jerusalem Center Websites

www.jcpa.org (English)
www.jcpa.org.il (Hebrew)
www.jcpa-lecape.org (French)
www.jer-zentrum.org (German)
www.facebook.com/jerusalemcenter
www.twitter.com/JerusalemCenter
www.youtube.com/TheJerusalemCenter

President - Dr. Dore Gold
Director General - Chaya Herskovic

Steering Committee:
Chairman - Dr. Manfred Gerstenfeld
Members - Prof. Rela Mintz Geffen
　　　　　　Prof. Arthur I. Eidelman
　　　　　　Zvi R. Marom
　　　　　　Prof. Yakir Plessner
　　　　　　Prof. Shmuel Sandler
　　　　　　Prof. Efraim Torgovnik